Jewellery
Diana Scarisbrick

The Costume Accessories Series
General Editor: Dr Aileen Ribeiro

B.T. BATSFORD LTD
LONDON

ISBN 0 7134 4278 6

Typeset by Tek-Art Ltd, Kent
and printed in Great Britain by
R J Acford,
Chichester, Sussex
for the publishers
B.T. Batsford Ltd
4 Fitzhardinge Street
London W1H 0AH

Contents

Acknowledgment

The author acknowledges with gratitude the help
given her by the following: Michael Dillon for his
advice on the history of dress, Peter Hinks for com-
menting on nineteenth- and twentieth-century
developments, and Barbara Scott, Rosalind Mazzawi,
Mary Fielden, Camilla Preston, Virginia Zervudachi,
Michael Bell and Rebecca Shaw for their kindness in
obtaining photographs.

List of Illustrations

Introduction

When considering the development of jewellery as a costume accessory, it is impossible to look at English jewels in isolation. French leadership in the design of clothes and accessories which has always influenced developments in England was recognized in the seventeenth century by Henry Peacham who complained in his book *The Truth of Our Times* (1638) that 'we cannot invent them ourselves but when one is grown stale runne over to France to seek a new making.' This ascendancy manifested itself in various ways. There was, for instance, a series of pattern books of jewel designs, beginning with the early examples of the jewelled *cosses de pois* bouquets of Balthasar Le Mersier in 1626, which diffused French styles abroad. Comparison with similar publications in England and Germany shows the reliance on Parisian prototypes which were either copied outright or modified to suit national taste. Then, from the reign of Marie de' Medicis, the French royal family set great store by the possession of jewellery: Anne of Austria's collection was so famous that the sculptor Bernini was taken to see it as one of the sights of Paris in 1665, while Louis XIV dazzled his court with the diamonds he wore as the personification of the Sun King. Another enthusiast was the Duc d'Orléans, and the jewels taken to Spain by his daughter Marie Louise d'Orléans on her marriage to Charles II in 1676 won French craftsmanship a great reputation there. Distinguished visitors such as the Electress Sophia of Hanover and the Duchess of Bracciano from Rome had their jewels remodelled while in France, being unhappy with the old hereditary settings amidst the novelty and sparkle of Versailles.

French court jewellers such as Montarsy gained international fame, and after the Revocation of the Edict of Nantes in 1685 so many goldsmiths emigrated that in 1706 the Duchesse d'Orléans declared that it was no longer true that nothing pretty could be obtained outside France, the best craftsmen being now in the northern capitals of Europe. Certainly the jewellery trade in eighteenth-century London numbered many firms of Huguenot origin — Chenevix, Harrache and Dutens for example, but their style was necessarily adapted to British taste, and Paris still remained the centre for all luxury items and jewellery in particular. The 1st Earl of Harcourt summed up the situation in a letter to his son dated 1756: 'We like their trifles but detest their government.' The publication of pattern books continued, foreign courts competed for the services of the best Parisian goldsmiths and the most successful — Ducrollay, Rondé and Jacquemin — were as celebrated as their predecessors at the court of Louis XIV. This was due to their genius not only for design but also for execution. Both diamonds and coloured stones were mounted in gold and silver settings of unrivalled finesse, the claws holding the stones being reduced in size so that the gems shone forth, seemingly independent of the metal framework. For clients such as Madame de Pompadour who liked to combine both light and colour G.F. Strass succeeded in tinting diamonds, as well as perfecting a formula for paste. This became a speciality of French craftsmen and much was exported. When the Rococo style succeeded the Baroque the initiative once more came from a French jeweller, identified as Augustin Duflos by J.H. Pouget. In the introduction to his book of jewellery designs, *Traité des Pierres Precieuses* (1762), Pouget attributes French supremacy in such matters to the national temperament — soft, charming and artistic — which created an atmosphere in which the rich foreigner could always be sure of finding agreeable ways of spending his money.

English memoirs of the time confirm this view. Women returning home from Paris were beseiged by their friends for information about the smartest way of wearing clothes and jewels and all were impressed by the French knack of making magnificence elegant. After an evening at the opera in Versailles in 1775 the Earl of Malmesbury wrote home 'the show which the French ladies always make above those of other nations added much to the spectacle — the ornaments of their headdress and their robes so disposed and varied composed a most beautiful tout ensemble.'

The Revolution of 1789 brought this situation to only a temporary halt for under Napoleon a new society emerged requiring *de luxe* parures, decorations and insignia and this revival of the art of jewellery was maintained by the 'Restauration' monarchy and emulated abroad. Even Louis Philippe, despite his cosy domestic image, spent large sums on jewellery and an inventory made by the Crown jeweller, Bapst, in 1839 lists seven different parures owned by Queen Amélie alone. Even greater developments accompanied the Second Empire which reintroduced all the pomp and display which had characterized the regime of Napoleon. Many of the Crown jewels were reset for the Empress Eugénie and those who thronged to the balls and receptions at the Tuileries and Compiègne imitated her style, much to the advantage of the jewellers, some of whom made fortunes. Under the Republic after 1870 firms such as Cartier, Boucheron and Chaumet continued from strength to strength, for a new element entered the market in the form of millionaires from North and South America with vast sums to spend. The great reputation of the French jewellers was further boosted by their success at the series of international exhibitions which followed the Great Exhibition held in London in 1851. The London and provincial jewellers, however competent, could not compete with the French and in any case English clients, being interested above all in intrinsic value, did not encourage artistry; they were happy with conventional designs provided the stones were of top quality and the workmanship substantial. The fashion correspondent of the *Illustrated London News*, which included reports from Paris from its first issue in 1842, also attributed French superiority to the fact that educationally the English jeweller compared unfavourably with his French counterpart.

When the reaction against stereotyped jewellery design came in the last decade of the nineteenth century it was again the French jewellers who rose to the occasion. On the one hand artists such as René Lalique and Henri Vever assumed the leadership of the Art Nouveau style, while Cartier and Boucheron initiated the use of platinum settings in diamond jewellery in Neo Classical styles of great beauty and refinement, perfectly in tune with Belle Epoque taste. To make sure of their empire they set up branches in New York and London, and at the holiday resorts of Biarritz, Deauville and Cannes.

The internationalization of French taste which resulted has continued throughout the twentieth century due to the extraordinary resilience of the dynasties reigning in the Place Vendôme and the Rue de la Paix. The Exposition des Arts Decoratifs in 1925 included jewels combining chic modernity with impeccable quality and French mastery of Art Deco remained unchallenged, accompanied by impressive technical achievements such as the invention of the invisible setting by Van Cleef and Arpels in 1937. They showed their vitality and enterprise again after 1945 in the production of elegant and sumptuous parures complementing the creations of *haute couture*. The memoirs of Christian Dior record the care with which he chose jewels to enhance the appeal of his clothes and in this respect he was acting in the long-standing French tradition — looking at jewels not just as investments or symbols but primarily as a means of beautifying the human person and therefore subject to the changing law of fashion.

1

Baroque Uniformity and Splendour
1600-1715

A new chapter in the history of jewellery opens in the seventeenth century, when instead of expressing ideas from myth and allegory in figurative compositions of enamelled goldwork, jewels were simplified into clusters of pearls, diamonds and precious stones, designed to highlight dress and hair.

The lead came from the court of Henri IV and Marie de' Medicis in France, and in spite of several years of civil war continued through to the reign of their grandson, Louis XIV (1643-1715), when the spirit of Baroque magnificence reached its apogee at Versailles. Paris was the centre for luxuries of all kinds including jewellery, and the French abroad, such as Madame d'Aulnoy who visited Spain in 1679, were struck by the poor quality of foreign work as well as its outdated design.[1] However, soon after, the emigration of Huguenot goldsmiths and jewellers following the revocation of the Edict of Nantes in 1685 brought French craftsmanship to the Protestant countries of northern Europe, particularly England. Parisian fashions had been introduced there much earlier, by Henrietta Maria, the French queen of Charles I. This ascendancy was further consolidated when the French nobility, deprived of political power by the absolutist government of Louis XIV, turned to gambling and the finer points of dress and etiquette for occupation and amusement. The standard at Versailles was set by Monsieur, the Duc d'Orléans, brother of the king and the personification of courtly elegance with his high heels, flame-coloured ribbons and diamond-spangled velvet mantle. With Jean Berain (1638-1711) as his personal designer, Monsieur's authority on matters of taste was recognized by all his relations including the Electress Sophia of Hanover who had her jewels reset on his advice. She came to Paris in 1679 for the marriage of his daughter, Marie Louise, to Charles II of Spain, and the bride's jewels, symbolizing the prestige of France, represented the stately Orléans style.[2]

These fashions, originating at court, and recorded in the paintings of Rubens, Van Dyck, Sir Peter Lely, Pierre Mignard and Nicolas de Largillière, were sub-

1 Queen Henrietta Maria (1609-69), by Anthony Van Dyck, c. 1632. The Queen wears pearls at the neck, across the shoulders in a rope looped over in front around a large diamond pendant hanging from a ribbon bow; a small gold and diamond brooch pins the edges of her lace collar together.

sequently adopted by burghers and merchants, who also affirmed their position in society by means of expensive clothes and personal ornaments. The general line of seventeenth-century women's costume was established in 1622 when Rubens painted the double portrait commemorating the marriages of Anne of Austria with Louis XIII, and Isabelle de Bourbon with the future Philip IV of Spain in 1615.[3] Jewellery accentuated the fashionable silhouette: full skirts laced at the front by ribbons terminating in jewelled points; the seams of the bodice and the tapering waistline outlined by brooches; a low neckline decorated by a large ornament set with precious stones; and billowing sleeves held in place by glittering clasps, with pearl earrings and necklaces, and coronets, bodkins and aigrettes for the hair.

This magnificent formula for court jewellery continued unaltered throughout the Baroque period, becoming richer during the reign of Louis XIV. Henrietta of England, the first wife of Monsieur, was painted in 1665 in the fashionable dress: a profusion of ruffles, flounces and ribbons with jewelled clusters clasping her slashed sleeves, and diamonds pinned in rows like braid across her stomacher, the edges of her deep lace collar joined together by a large breast jewel.[4] The French royal family spent a fortune on their jewels, and courtiers received them from the king as lottery prizes, and as gifts at christenings, weddings and New Year's Day. Madame de Maintenon, who married Louis XIV at a secret ceremony in 1684, advised the young Duchess of Burgundy to take more trouble over her looks and added 'it is important for you to wear jewels so as to draw attention to the clearness of your skin and the neatness of your figure.'[5] In accordance with the principles of Baroque art, jewellery and dress were conceived as part of an ensemble to impress and sparkle at long range and in these circumstances the diamond emerged as the dominant factor. The enterprising merchant G.B. Tavernier imported fabulous gems and jewels from the East and the opening of the mines of the Golconda group in Deccan, India ensured a regular supply of stones of quality so that by 1661 Robert de Berghen commented on the number of Indian dealers buying in Europe.[6] At the same time the discovery of the laws of refraction and the principles of analytical geometry stimulated progress in facetting and polishing in the traditional centres of Antwerp and Amsterdam, and also in Paris, where diamond-cutters were established by the mid-seventeenth century. The rose cut with multiple facets was a great advance on the point and table-cut diamond, and the full-cut brilliant appeared on the market soon after the death

of Cardinal Mazarin (1602-61). His passion for precious stones was shared by the rich and royal of Europe, and although the diamond ranked first, coloured stones – chrysolites, topazes, turquoises coral and opals as well as the more valuable sapphires, emeralds and rubies – were also prized. Progress in facetting affected these too, for there are a few references to cabochon stones in inventories of this period. Pearls tripled in price over 60 years according to de Berghen, and were worn in the hair, and next to the skin: around the wrists, hung around the neck or from the ears, in drop-shaped shoulder clasps, or attached to velvet bands at the throat.

Substitutes were on sale in Paris by 1657 and John Evelyn, visiting Venice in 1645, saw 'the famous lapidaries for false stones and pastes, Marco Terrasse and Gilbert', while Robert de Berghen also mentions the manufacture of every kind of precious stone. In England the crystals mined in Cornwall, near Harrogate, and near Bristol[7], were set in rings and earrings, but the flint glass produced by George Ravenscroft in 1675 was considered superior. All sections of society wore paste jewellery – Anne of Austria had a pair of ruby earrings, one of them imitation, and Queen Henrietta Maria of England owned marcasite jewels as well as a cross set with glass sapphires. The best market for paste was Spain where Madame d'Aulnoy was surprised to find ladies of the first rank loading themselves with 'false stones which they buy at dear rates and when I asked them why they were so fond of these counterfeit diamonds they told me it was because they could have them as big as they desired.' Some were indeed as big as eggs and were set in necklaces twisted round the neck like great ropes of onions. The quantities of pearls used everywhere in Europe for jewellery, embroidered on clothes, threaded into torsades to emphasize seams and necklines, created a demand for imitations and these too were imported from Venice. The firm of Jacqui established in France in 1686 went on making artificial pearls right up to the Second Empire of Napoleon III.

Robert de Berghen also advised jewellers on the best way to set both artificial and genuine stones. The settings were now much reduced in scale instead

---

2 Marie Adelaide de Savoie, Duchess of Burgundy ▷
(1685-1712), by J.B. de Santerre, 1709. The front of the bodice is embellished with a set of jewelled brooches of graduated size imitating the frogging on the jackets of Prussian soldiers.

of emphasized with ornaments derived from classical architecture and sculpture, and for the backs and borders he recommended white enamel to be used with coloured stones, black with diamonds. The object of design was to give the eye the illusion of masses of stones assembled independently of a containing metal frame, blazing with light and fire. Although the Spanish preferred gold settings, elsewhere these were reserved for coloured stones, diamonds and crystals being set in silver which presented less of a challenge to their white brilliance.

Enamel continued to provide the main means of decoration for watches and miniature cases and French craftsmen excelled in this medium. The Toutin family perfected a technique whereby a surface of opaque white or blue enamel could be applied on gold, serving as a base for a wide range of colours reproducing bouquets of flowers, or narrative paintings by Baroque artists such as Simon Vouet. Another type of enamel-

3 *Design for jewelled bouquet by Balthasar Le Mersier, Paris 1626. This type of stylized leaf interpreted in enamelled gold and stones is called cosses de pois or peapod ornament.*

ling was the speciality of Blois, where craftsmen such as the Legaré family used it for framing cameos and miniatures with wreaths of fruit and flowers in high relief. Gilles Legaré, court jeweller, published designs in this style in 1663 which include plaques for bracelets and chains combining enamelled floral motifs with diamonds and coloured stones in silver and gold leaf-shaped settings.

It was by means of these engravings that French taste was diffused throughout Europe. According to the *Mercure Galant* (founded 1672), fashionable people had their jewels reset every two or three years, and although few jewels survived continual restyling, the patterns for them still exist and provide a reliable chronological sequence of design. Sets of engravings such as *Bouquets d'Orfèvrerie*, published in 1626 by Balthasar Le Mersier, and later those by François Lefebvre (1665) mirror the contemporary passion for botany, likewise expressed in tapestries, marquetry and still life painting. The earliest floral and foliate designs are based on a pea pod plant called *cosses de pois* with sprays of leaves curling round petal-shaped settings, but by mid-century a more naturalistic style emerged which is represented by the patterns of Jean Vauquer of Blois. Acanthus leaves, richly curved and intricate, were the theme of the engravings published by Louis Roupert of Metz (1668) and others by Theodore Le Juge.

The amount of jewellery worn on the head reached such proportions during the reign of Louis XIV that in March 1692 Madame de Maintenon attributed the collapse of the slender young Duchesse de Maine to the weight of the gold and gems in her hair. As in the Renaissance period, strings of pearls were threaded like ribbon through plaited and piled up hair, and at her wedding in 1697 the Duchess of Burgundy wore her ringlets braided with pearls and rubies and in a net so thickly covered with diamonds that few could bear to look at her. At the candlelit reception afterwards the mirrored reflections of the diamonds blazing from the hair and dress made the Galerie des Glaces seem brighter than the midday sun. Strands of gems were tied at the crown of the head by a ribbon bow, fixed by a small jewelled brooch or an aigrette of cut stones.

The fashion for aigrettes was introduced by Henri IV who wore one in his hat, and his wife Marie de'Medicis who placed not only jewelled feathers and flowers but other motifs such as a crowned heart wounded by arrows, at the side of her head. Plumes of rubies and emeralds held by crescents and coronets were designed by Arnold Lulls, jeweller to James I and Anne of Denmark, and the designs of Pierre

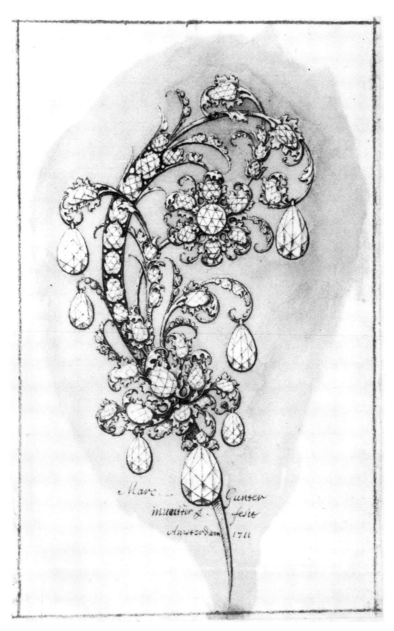

Marchant – *Feuillages d'Orfèvrerie, Bouquets et Medaillons* (1623) included jewelled *cosses de pois* bouquets for the hair. Later, naturalistic caterpillars and snails crept into the compositions and the effect of flashing light and fresh bright colours in the hair was enhanced by tremblers (stem-like springs) which shook with the wearer's movements. Only the very richest women could wear the sprays of diamond and pearl flowers fashionable at Versailles after 1689, for to look right a large quantity of stones was required.

4 Design for an aigrette by Marcus Gunter, 1711. Only the richest could afford hair ornaments of this importance, designed to display large rose-cut and briolette diamonds.

Mlle d'Orléans was admired when she wore one of these bouquets of diamonds and pearls clasping three feathers in her hair, dyed to match the ribbons at her throat. Jewels of this rich Baroque style were a

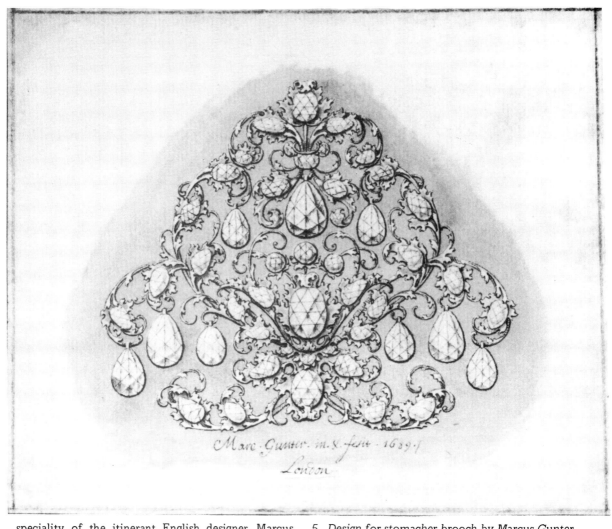

Marc. Gunter. in.x. fecit. 1689.

London

speciality of the itinerant English designer, Marcus Gunter (1684-1733). This Leicestershire painter travelled from one town to another in Europe, making his living designing jewels, decorations and other ornaments.[8]

Men had given up aigrettes by 1691 when Liselotte, the second wife of the Duc d'Orléans, wrote to her aunt the Electress Sophia of Hanover:

> I can't think who could have told the Elector of Brandenbourg that diamond aigrettes are worn in the hats here — nobody young or old does except perhaps a dancer at the Opera — I therefore cannot send you any patterns. I can, however, tell you that the feathers in the hat are fixed by a buckle of brilliants in the front, and the brim with a sort of loop set with large diamonds.[9]

For most of the seventeenth century men encircled

5 *Design for stomacher brooch by Marcus Gunter, London 1689. Large, rose-cut diamonds are set in a symmetrical composition of acanthus leaves in a stomacher for wear in the front of the dress at the neckline.*

the crown of the hat with jewelled bands, but when upturned brims became fashionable they were held in place by jewelled loops, the most celebrated being the diamond bow with the Peregrina pearl in the centre worn by Charles II of Spain.

Less ambitious were the bodkins which women put in their hair, the long pins topped with decorative heads. Two bodkins were found in the hoard of Jacobean and Stuart jewellery discovered at Cheapside and now in the London Museum, one decorated with a diamond and topaz flower head, the other with a garnet shepherd's crook. A jewelled ship bodkin impressed the Italian artist Gian Lorenzo Bernini when he was shown the jewels of Anne of Austria as one of the sights of Paris in 1665. Women liked to think of their hair shining like the starry sky at night, and therefore sprinkled it with as many ornaments as they possessed. Marie Louise d'Orléans owned a great

6 *Gold and diamond necklace and girandole or branch earrings, c. 1690. Facetted diamonds glittering in sober gold settings were now considered sufficiently splendid independent of enamelled ornament.*

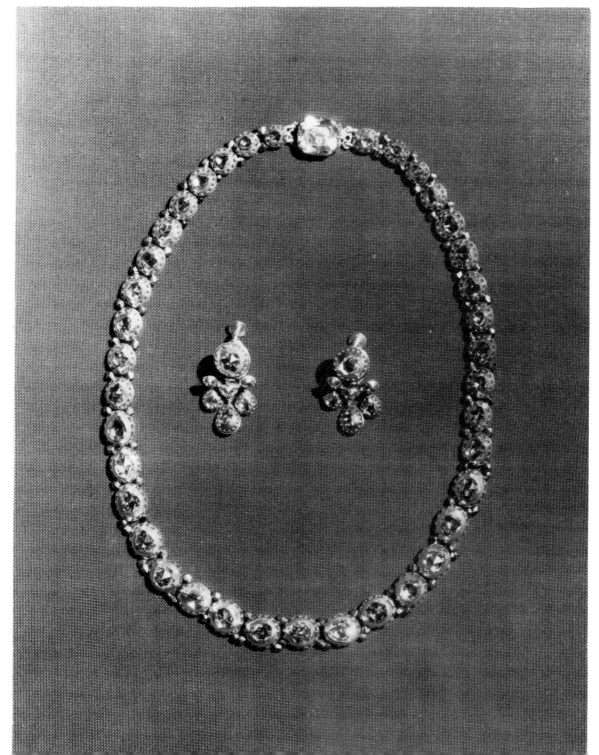

selection: gold and diamond rosettes with enamelled backs, snails, caterpillars and butterflies perched on long plants, and the name of her husband Charles II, King of Spain, inscribed in diamonds. Madame d'Aulnoy commented on the excessive number of bodkins worn in Spain, and in France the Duchesse de Berri appeared in full dress with more than 14 bodkins set with the 'most splendid diamonds in the world'. Pendant drop hair jewels with diamond earrings *en suite* were considered very grand and the Queen of Spain asked her friends in Paris in 1708 to find a briolette to pin in the midst of her hair to match the long earrings which she wore on full-dress court occasions.

Earrings, which had only a limited appeal in the sixteenth century, were in fashion for almost all the Baroque period. Marie de'Medicis wore them and Arnold Lulls designed several models — compositions of coloured stones and diamond crescents, snakes and clusters of grapes; amethyst earrings designed as bunches of grapes were found in the Cheapside hoard. Later designs such as those made by Paul Maréchal for Anne of Austria are complex and substantial arrangements of bows, ribbons, crowns and bouquets branching out from a top cluster, and are called girandole, after the branch-like forms of candlesticks and chandeliers. Girandole earrings showed off pearls and diamonds to advantage, especially briolettes which hung transparent so the light reflected from both the front and back as they swung with the head. The eye was drawn to the face thus lit up, and it was by means of her emerald earrings that Madame de

7 *Gold necklace enamelled in sepia monochrome, back and front, mid-seventeeth century. The plaques are enamelled on the front with topographical scenes alternating with allegorical figures of the Virtues, and on the back with botanical motifs.*

FRONT

BACK

Soubise signalled to Louis XIV (whose gift they were) that her husband had left for Paris and they were free to rendezvous.[10] Coloured stones were usually foiled and close set with the white backs enamelled *a la porcelana* with polychrome flowers and patterns for them were published by Gilles Legaré.[11] Madame d'Aulnoy was astonished by the length and weight of the earrings worn in Spain – 'longer than one's hands and so heavy that I have wondered how they could carry them without tearing out the holes in their ears.' As many as 13 hinged sections, each studded with diamonds and emeralds, hung down tier by tier. Jet tear-shaped pendant earrings were worn for mourning both in Spain and elsewhere, and inventories such as that of Beatrix de Cusance[12] list earrings with *memento mori* devices – hourglasses, pairs of coffins, and death's heads in enamelled gold.

Drop-shaped pearls were naturally suited for earrings and their colour and sheen blended well with the skin. Matching pairs of large size and quality such as those given by Louis XIV to Marie Mancini made truly royal gifts, and men also liked them, but worn singly. Charles I went to the scaffold with a large pearl hanging from one ear, and Louis Roupert is portrayed similarly adorned in the frontispiece of his collection of engraved designs. Smaller pearls of round and even shape were linked into tassels, and earrings of this type were published by Francois Lefebvre.

Women wore single or multiple rows of pearls around the neck, the centre emphasized by a pear-drop pendant or jewelled locket. Necklaces of diamonds or coloured stones were set in heavy gold or silver collets enamelled *a la porcelana* at the back, and tied with coloured ribbons, and the ribbon motif was adopted for necklaces. Cheaper versions in paste were made so well that thieves could be deceived by them, and as an alternative to gem stones and pearls, plaques enamelled with landscapes or figures, or stamped in relief in gold, were linked together. An innovation was described by the Marquis de Dangeau on 3 March 1688 – the *coulant* or slide attached to the silk ribbon at the neck with pendant cross.[13] Besides crosses, other emblems of symbolic character were worn in this way, including stars, butterflies, doves and sheaves of corn.

So often were the great ladies of the time painted with chains of gold, diamonds and pearls hanging across the bosom, or baldric-wise over the shoulder, that they must be included in any account of seventeenth-century women's jewellery. Marie Louise d'Orléans owned several which are described in her inventory and their main decorative feature was the complementary glitter of table and rose-cut diamonds, combined with enamelled snails and rosettes. Chains of black ambergris beads alternating with death's heads with diamond eye sockets or diamond-cut jet were worn with matching earrings for mourning. Although agates, cornelians and onyxes which take a high polish were liked for their strong colours and the contrast of opaque and transparent layers, engraved stones were most sought after and Dorothy Osborne refers to them in a letter to her lover, the diplomat Sir William Temple: 'I have sent to Italy for seals – 'tis a humour which your old acquaintance Mr Smith and his lady have brought up – they say she wears twenty strung on a ribbon, like the nuts boys play withal.'[14] The subject matter of the engraved gems in these chains is often linked thematically – illustrations of classical legends or miniature portrait galleries of kings and queens. The painter Rubens, who had a fine collection of engraved gems, had some of them set in the bracelets which his wife Isabella wears in their double portrait at the Munich Pinakotek.

Being the standard reward for loyal service, chains were proof of a man's official status as well as his wealth. George Villiers, 1st Duke of Buckingham, as representative of Charles I for the proxy marriage with Henrietta Maria in Paris in 1625, cut a dash with his white velvet suits hung with ropes of pearls. Most men wore chains of wrought gold, some imported from abroad – Ben Jonson alludes to the 'Savoy chain' in his comedy *The New Inn* (1629), and a complicated pattern of rosette links came from China. Value was determined by the length and richness of the links, and on his mission to Sweden in 1653 Ambassador Whitelocke had trouble with some of his suite who complained that their chains were not good enough.[15] His own personal gift from Queen Christina was 'a case of gold fairly enamelled and having in the midst of it the picture of the Queen done to the life and very like set round with twelve large diamonds with twelve small between.' Medallic or miniature portraits were often presented with the chains and preserved in the Ashmolean Museum, Oxford, are the chains and medallions representing the King of Denmark and the Elector of Brandenbourg given to Elias Ashmole in 1674 and 1678 respectively. These badges of royal approval were part of ambassadorial dress, and Lady Fanshawe described her husband Richard going to his audience with the King of Spain in 1665 with 'a rich and curious wrought gold chain made in the Indies at which hung the king his master's picture richly set in diamonds.'[16] All courtiers aspired to membership of the Orders of Chivalry and

the enamelled gold and jewelled collars, chains and insignia of the Garter, Golden Fleece and other Orders were made to a superb standard.

The changing fashions in jewels of the Baroque period can be best followed in the design of jewels for the breast. These made suitable wedding presents since no fashionable wardrobe was complete without them. A large, golden, diamond-studded ornament resembling a stylized plant, now in the Victoria and Albert Museum, is similar to the designs of Jacques Caillart, a contemporary of Balthasar Le Mersier and represents the *cosses de pois* style.[17] This style evolved into more naturalistic compositions with insects and mixed flowers individualized by coloured stones and enamel, the long stems tied with ribbons.

8 George Villiers, 1st Duke of Buckingham (1592-1628), by Michiel van Miereveld, 1625. The profusion of pearls sewn on fabric, hanging in ropes beneath the lace collar and girdling the waist illustrates the extravagant style with which George Villiers dazzled his contemporaries.

9 Gold medals and chains, one of filigree, the other ▷ of plain open links, 1674 and 1678. Elias Ashmole wears the openwork filigree chain, originally consisting of 71 links, in his portrait by John Riley (1682).

Marie Louise d'Orléans owned many brooches of this kind, the backs enamelled with black, white and purple flowers, and the fronts heavily jewelled; a bouquet of lilies and carnations hanging from a rosette and framed in interlaced ribbons was set with 245 diamonds, 287 rubies and 128 emeralds.

The possession of gems signified status and the jewels that displayed them were often no more than mere clusters whose size counted for more than design, sometimes with pendant stones or drop-shaped pearls attached. Heirlooms were paraded in this way and such was their prestige that each generation tried to ensure that they remained in the family as emblems of dynastic pride. Progress in cutting which released the brilliance and quality of fine stones and emphasized their size coincided with Baroque taste for the

10 Polychrome enamel and jewelled bouquet of flowers arranged round a flaming heart held in two hands, second half of the seventeenth century. In this period designs were more naturalistic, and the colours of the enamel and stones match the flowers represented; butterflies and bees perch on petals fitted with springs which would seem to be blown by the wind as the wearer moved.

11 Mary II, Queen of England (1662-94), by William ▷ Wissing. The Queen wears pearls in her ears and at the throat, her sleeves are clasped with jewelled cluster brooches and the neckline is embellished with a large diamond stomacher brooch.

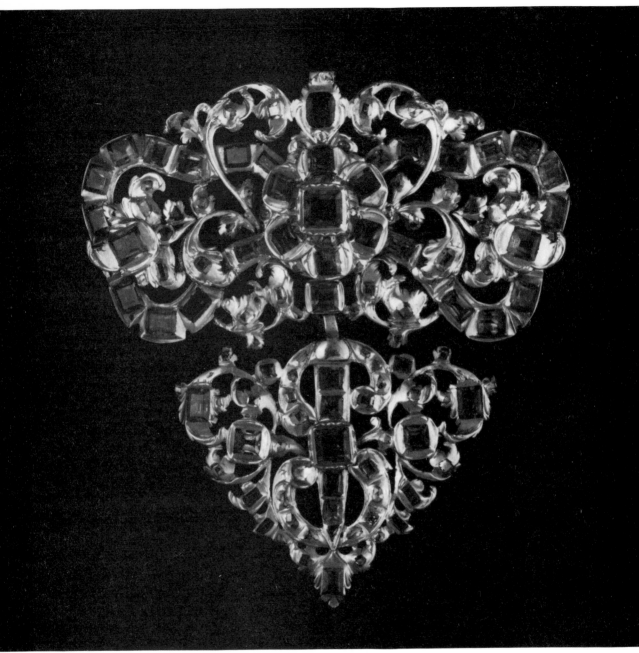

12 *Gold and emerald stomacher brooch, Spanish,*
second half of the seventeenth century. The barred
S motif is a rebus for Esclavo, denoting membership
of a religious confraternity. Emerald devotional
jewels of this type are characteristic of Spanish
Baroque taste.

grand, as represented by a jewel owned by Mary II,
wife of William III of Orange: 'a great jewel of diamonds to be worn before with a large heart diamond
in the middle thereof.' This could have had a sentimental significance since she also wore a large rose
diamond hanging from a ruby ribbon, the back
enamelled with the ciphers W and M, and inscribed
'L'AMOUR EN EST LE LIEN'. [18] Marie Louise

d'Orléans also owned a jewel composed of her cipher and that of her husband Charles II interlaced, and a series of hearts (winged, crowned and wounded by arrows) and even Cupid himself, with bow, wings, quiver and arrow studded with diamonds, rubies and emeralds.

Spanish cipher jewels were also devotional – IHS, the abbreviated form of Jesus Hominum Salvator, MA for Maria, and S for Esclavo, indicating the membership of a religious confraternity. Miniature tableaux of angels venerating the Host and the dove of the Holy Spirit enamelled white with its breast set with crystals or diamonds were made into pendants to wear on the breast. Because of their simple outlines both Jerusalem and Latin crosses were the ideal medium for the display of real and counterfeit gems. While for some the cross was an affirmation of religious faith, others regarded it as a mere ornament; Liselotte d'Orléans comments in a letter to the Electress Sophia in 1688 'people are wearing diamond crosses – not for devotional reasons but to dress themselves up'. She may have remembered this at the wedding of the Duke and Duchess of Burgundy in 1697 when many older women wore rich diamond crosses with gold-embroidered black velvet dresses.

In the second half of the seventeenth century the bow knot was the most characteristic breast jewel, evolving from silk ribbons trimming the neckline and pinned with jewelled clusters and crosses, and finally executed in gold and gemstones. Originating thus as a dress trimming, jewelled bows always harmonized with clothes, and although their name, 'Sevigné', associates them with the gifted letter writer, Madame de Sevigné (1626-96), who wears one in her portrait by Robert Nanteuil, they appear in portraits as early as the 1640s when they were known as 'galants'. The basic design could be varied according to the number of loops and in 1663 Gilles Legaré published several graceful versions, close in style to a jewel in the Rijksmuseum, Amsterdam, which has the front set with rubies and pearls, and the back enamelled with tulips.[19] A *de luxe* development of the bow-knot theme is represented by a jewelled cravat decorated with bow knots, probably made in Paris, presented in 1679 to the Shrine of Our Lady of the Pillar in Saragossa; it is now in the Victoria and Albert Museum. Towards the end of the century ribbons were combined with acanthus scrolls in openwork designs outlined by the densely textured dress fabric beneath.

Brandenbourgs were another type of jewel derived from costume. Always in fashion, the Duc d'Orléans was described by the *Mercure Galant* at a fete in 1677 'wearing stones set in designs like the frogging on

13 *Enamelled gold and diamond breast ornament, French, second half of the seventeenth century. This was presented in 1679 to the Shrine of Our Lady of the Pillar in Saragossa and simulates a lace-edged cravat pinned with a series of bow knots set with table diamonds. It demonstrates the delicacy with which the French jeweller combined diamonds with enamel.*

Brandenbourg soldiers' jackets.' He wore them again in 1692 at the marriage of his son, the Duc de Châtres, and the black velvet suit designed for the bridegroom by Jean Berain was also enriched with diamond brandenbourgs. Designs were published by François Lefebvre and Theodore Lejuge, and brandenbourgs were worn either in rows of graduated size, or as one important jewel in the front of the dress by women, including the Duchess of Burgundy, their military character contrasting with her girlish looks.

Exhausted by the weight of the Crown jewels borrowed for her part in the tragedy *Absolon* in 1702, the Duchess of Burgundy had to retire to bed; in accordance with the Baroque principle of unity, even jewellery in such a quantity would have been designed as a set. Clusters, bows, and bouquets pinned on the skirt, bodice and sleeves highlighted the opulent fabrics, and some early designs were figurative. Queen Henrietta Maria had matching brooches of golden eagles or amorini with rose diamond breasts and other women wore them too, including the Countess of

14 *Angela Maria Lombardi, School of Rome, c.*
1710. This aristocratic Roman lady wears a single
brandenbourg of diamonds and pearls at the neck-
line with pendant attached, a pearl necklace with
slide and cross, pearl bracelets tied with ribbon bows,
diamond and pearl drop earrings, a solitaire ring and
in her hair one large and several small bodkins.

Cleveland, and Catherine Bruce who has them pinned
across the bodice in her miniature by Samuel Cooper.
Sometimes a single such brooch adorned the centre
of the neckline, linked by golden chains to smaller
versions on the shoulders, though these and the sleeves
were more usually clasped with simple clusters or
girandoles of diamonds, pearls and coloured stones.
The close relationship of jewels with dress is confirmed

in another letter from Liselotte to the Electress Sophia, dated 1 November 1679: 'This is a good moment to send you the diamond studs from the King – Monsieur is very sorry he cannot show you himself how they should be worn on the dress or sleeves, but he has already conferred with Madame de Mecklenburg who will send you a paper pattern.'

Buttons were one of the means by which men's clothing was enriched and expensive sets were given as wedding presents by bride to bridegroom. Ambassador Whitelocke was proud of the 'very fair diamond buttons' on the black English cloth suit he wore to his first audience with Queen Christina and also with the rubies in enamelled gold buttons which he kept for his last meeting with her. Louis XIV and Monsieur were almost never seen in public with less than several millions worth of buttons, and at the wedding of the Comte de Toulouse the Duc de Maine wore buttons of golden anemones with his grey and white suit. Inventories sometimes indicate the designs of women's buttons, plain gold being worked into similar naturalistic designs of leaves and flowers. Travelling to Nottingham, Celia Fiennes noticed the flourishing industry of glass buttons – cheap substitutes for the rich diamond sets worn by royalty and courtiers. Pairs of linked buttons fastened the cuff at the wrist instead of ribbons. Designs show some variety, although the most frequent type was square, set with crystal and the back enamelled *a la porcelana* with acanthus and flowers.

Buckles, placed prominently in the hat, garters and shoes, were sometimes very luxurious and were worn by women according to Mary Evelyn in her satire *Mundus Muliebris* in 'shoe, cloak and stays as well as girdle'. The waist could be emphasized by other means besides a buckle – Anne of Austria owned a diamond-studded black velvet belt and in Holland rich women liked the contrast of golden girdles terminating in openwork pomanders against their sober, rich, dark clothing. The Duchesse de Longueville was painted by Van Dyck with her waist and low décolletage outlined with torsades of pearls, each swag alternating with a large jewelled cluster. Spanish women liked *de luxe* versions of the rope belts of the Franciscan or Carmelite friars, transforming them into gold with diamond-studded knots. Northern taste preferred allusions to the pleasures of hunting, in belts made from plaques decorated with vignettes of the chase in the difficult technique of *émail en résille sur verre*. All the items required for refined living – fans, watches, seals, scissor and knife cases – hung from the belt attached by golden chains to a 'crochet'.

Bracelets were usually strands of pearls, or silk and velvet ribbons tied in bow knots, or running through a slide of an emblematic or commemorative character. Anne of Austria wore a miniature case in the centre of a bracelet of polychrome enamelled gold, and Henrietta d'Orléans, the first wife of Monsieur, had the picture of her favourite pug, Mimi, set round with 20 little diamonds on her wrist. Beatrix de Cusance liked clasps ornamented with religious subjects – the Holy Shroud of Besançon, and a 'Veronica' (the image of Christ's face on the veil of St Veronica, Rome). In England emblems of this kind were usually of political significance and after the exile of James II in 1688 supporters of the Stuarts wore Jacobite jewellery decorated with his portrait, cipher and white rose. Inventories list jewelled clasps and even strands of diamonds and coloured stones but pearls were always the most sought after. Liselotte, Duchesse d'Orléans, was pleased with the wedding present of the Duc de Lorraine to her daughter in October 1698 – two bracelets, each composed of five rows of pearls a little larger than sugar peas, and pronounced them quite perfect. She did not wear bracelets herself, explaining 'they are only worn by people who make a point of showing off their pretty arms and hands – as I am not endowed I never wear mine, but carry them in my pocket in a case specially prepared for them.'

Liselotte did not wear topazes either, not because they did not suit her, but because Monsieur had given them all to his daughter Marie Louise when she married the King of Spain. They were one of the seven parures she owned, and these suites matching in stones and design became an established category of jewellery during the reign of Louis XIV. The parure of diamonds given by the king to Mademoiselle d'Aubigné, niece of Madame de Maintenon, on her marriage in 1698 and supplied by the jeweller Montarsy, consisted of the following items: a pair of earrings, a pair of pendants, a large loop, two sleeve loops, 16 sleeve clasps, 32 buttons, and a bow knot. The funeral parure of Frances Stuart, Duchess of Richmond, still preserved in Westminster Abbey illustrates the English style at the turn of the century: necklace with double loop in front, pair of drop earrings, sleeve clasps and brandenbourg *en suite*. Parures such as these contributed to the brilliance of social life. When the Marquis de Dangeau gave a dinner for the Duke of Mantua in 1704 he was delighted with his women guests whose jewellery not only enhanced their good looks but made his table sparkle. After another party in 1705 he observed how much better stones looked on women in the parures specially designed to show off the feminine face and figure.

2

Elegance and Sentiment
1715-1789

Women now became the principal medium for jewellery which, like carriages and retainers, was part of the state of the rich and well born. The high standards prevailing in all branches of the decorative arts were also applied to jewellery, which reached a level of artistry rarely equalled since. Taking stylistic elements at first from Rococo and then from Neo Classicism, designers maximized to the full the beauty of diamonds and coloured stones revealed by improved facetting. Exemplifying these developments was the Regent, the 137-carat Golconda diamond of the first water (highest quality) which was shaped as a brilliant between the years 1707 and 1717 with 58 beautifully proportioned facets distributing light evenly over the wide surface, and was subsequently acquired for the French Crown jewels. Thereafter, though table and rose-cuts continued in use, the better stones were brilliant-cut and the prestige of the diamond eclipsed pearls as well as other stones. Supplementing the traditional supply from Golconda were gems from Ninas in Brazil where diamond mines were in operation after the 1730s.

Those with technical knowledge led the field of design, which according to the Jean Bourguet[1] as early as 1723 was determined by the quantity and size of diamonds to be worked into settings. Augustin Duflos later declared in the preface to his published designs[2] that success depended on the quality of setting which could show inexpensive stones to greater effect than others more intrinsically valuable. He considered such expertise to result from practical experience of the gems and metals, allied to a sense of beauty based on the study of nature. French preeminence continued, and J.H. Prosper Pouget, proprietor of the Paris shop Le Bouquet de Diamants, affirmed in his introduction to *Traité des Pierres Precieuses* (1762) that the French certainly won the prize for taste in jewellery. Not only the designs of Bourguet, Duflos, and Pouget but others by Mondon, Lucotte, Maria and Babel and de la Cour were copied all over Europe, and itinerant craftsmen took both styles and working methods abroad. According to the

Duchesse d'Orléans in 1706 it was no longer true that nothing pretty could be made outside France, for, as she explained in a letter, the Protestants who had been driven out after the revocation of the Edict of Nantes had been the best craftsmen, and were now established in Germany and England. Other French jewellers besides Huguenots accepted invitations to work for foreign royalty: Augustin Duflos in Madrid, J.F. Fistaine in Copenhagen for Christian VII, and Louis Duval in St Petersburg for the Empress Catherine. In England Lady Pomfret acknowledged the superiority of the French jewellers when she tried to bribe Alphonse, the valet of her daughter's suitor, Lord Lincoln, with a diamond jabot pin: 'the trinket is prettily set, you will observe such workmanship as only jewellers of your nation can accomplish.'[3]

The marriage with Lord Lincoln never took place, and instead Sophy Pomfret became Lady Carteret, and in another letter her mother proudly alludes to her jewellery: 'the weight of her diamonds yesterday at the Drawing Room was I think one of the causes of her headache — her husband would not be pleased unless she was magnificent — he would have her covered with jewels, he would buy up all the lace in London to put it on her, he takes such pride in her beauty and so much trouble about her adornment Sophy would be culpable not to humour him.' The wearing of jewels in such quantities continued until the reign of Louis XVI, when his queen, Marie Antoinette, gave the stamp of royal approval to looser and less ceremonious toilettes, including the *chemise de la Reine,* an unshaped bodice open down the front, meeting at the centre and held in place by a sash. However, corsetted bodices, flattened busts, slim waists and large hoops continued in fashion all through the eighteenth century and only vanished with the French Revolution in 1789. In the Rococo period fabrics were less solemn and heavily patterned, culminating in the plain satins, soft light silks, taffetas and muslins of the Louis XVI style.

A distinction was made between full dress for public engagements and informal private wear, due to

15 *Empress Maria Theresa of Austria (1717-80), by
J.E. Liotard. Clusters of diamonds pinned in a band
encircling the crown of the black lace cap give sparkle
to her features.*

16 *Diamond and blue enamel aigrette, second half of the eighteenth century; designed as a bunch of peacock feathers with each 'eye' represented by a diamond in open setting amidst pavé-set diamonds in closed settings, the centre of each plume outlined in blue enamel.*

Sold at ye Queenshead & Star in St Martins Le Grand.   Publish'd according to

17 *Designs for jewellery by Thomas Flach, 1736. Symmetrical ribbonwork styles designed to carry quantities of coloured stones or diamonds.*

improvements in domestic lighting which meant that the major social events — plays, operas, masquerades, balls and card assemblies — could take place by night; since it was thought vulgar to parade expensive jewellery by day, diamond ornaments were reserved for candlelight occasions, while 'undress' jewellery was created for daytime cotton and wool fabrics. Not much jewellery is worn in portraits except by royalty and it is the published designs which provide the most accurate picture of the changing sequence of styles which begin with the designs of Marcus Gunter[4] and Thomas Flach.[5] They illustrate standardized versions of seventeenth-century types — aigrettes, butterflies and moths for the hair, girandole earrings, Sevigné

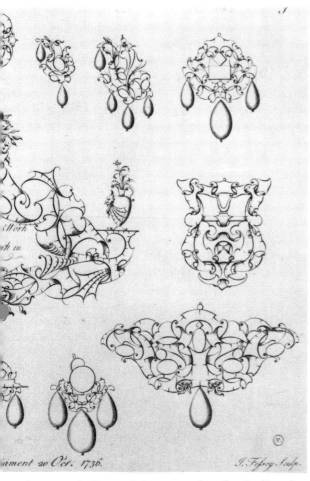

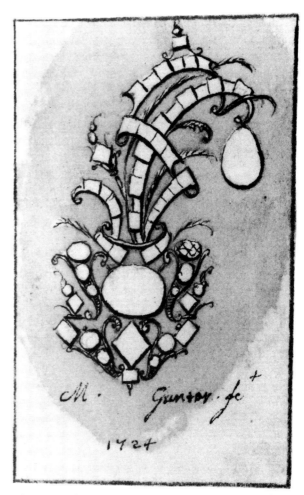

18 *Design for an aigrette by Marcus Gunter, 1724. The asymmetrical design and the absence of acanthus foreshadows the lighter rococo style.*

bows and diamond bouquets for the bodice; but whereas Thomas Flach in 1736 maintained a strictly symmetrical style, softened by a more liberal use of ribbonwork, Marcus Gunter by 1724 heralded the Rococo style by introducing asymmetrical compositions and discarding acanthus foliage. Pouget attributed the creation of Rococo jewellery to Duflos who in the late 1720s substituted naturalistic forms for the black enamel, heavy outlines and massive scrollwork of Baroque design. The change in style is first expressed in floral motifs which were individualized and grouped into bouquets modelled in relief instead of flat, the stones held unobtrusively by claws and massed into pavé settings. Colour effects similar to those in textiles were achieved by foiling, and even diamonds were successfully tinted by G.F. Strass in Paris, attracting the patronage of Madame de Pompadour.

This brilliant and elegant style was brought to perfection by the jeweller Lempereur, and it is also a characteristic of those pieces which after 1761 were designed 'á la Grecque' with classical fret, honeysuckle and husks in symmetrical and geometrical outlines.

Diamonds were set in silver, coloured stones in gold, and settings were both open and closed, some jewels combining both types. They were no longer enamelled at the back, the last designs of this kind being by the Augsburg designer F.J. Morisson, dated 1693, and he also gave alternatives in engraved gold. Enamelled decoration of great refinement was applied to the cases of watches, chatelaines, miniature frames and bracelet clasps, and in the last decades of the eighteenth century royal blue enamel was used to outline the rims of settings, or to cover plaques for

D.CARLOTA
PRINCEZA
DOBRASIL.

19 Dona Carlotta of Brazil, Portuguese School, late eighteenth century. *The miniature of her husband John VI of Portugal (1769-1826) bordered in diamonds hangs round her neck, and a London-made watch is prominently displayed on a chatelaine at the waist.*

20 Tsarina Maria Feodorovna (married to the future Paul I in 1776), by A. Roslin. *The head with hair dressed high in a pinnacle festooned with pearls and pinned with jewelled bouquets, feathers or Roman candles, was the culminating point of pre-Revolutionary eighteenth-century elegance.*

21 Silver and paste ornaments, second half of the eighteenth century. The high quality of design which characterizes paste jewellery is due to society patronage.

bracelets and rings, the deep colour contrasting splendidly with the gold. An enamel suite bought by the Contesse du Nord, Maria Feodorovna, wife of the future Tsar Paul I, during their visit to Paris in 1781-2, although framed in marcasite, was more expensive than diamond jewellery according to her lady in waiting, the Baronne d'Oberkirch.[6]

The increased cost of metal and stones owing to demand from the bourgeois class as well as the nobility stimulated the search for acceptable substitutes. Pinchbeck and similor were alloys of metal (copper and zinc) used instead of gold, and the quality of paste was so good that Horace Walpole, complaining in 1776 about the poor standard of modern stained glass, wondered why this was so, when every necklace-seller sold rubies and emeralds which jewellers had to take out of settings to ascertain whether they were genuine or not. The French excelled in this branch of jewellery too, and by 1767 the Corporation des Bijoutiers Faussetiers in France numbered 300, much of their production being for export. Pouget said that G.F. Strass perfected the formula for transparent flint glass which resembled diamonds when cut and facetted, and his rival Chéron successfully imitated rubies, emeralds, topazes and sapphires. Another source was Venice where turquoise paste was made of a quality considered more beautiful than the genuine stone. Although the English mastered the art of making the material at an early date, colouring was much inferior to French workmanship, as was cutting, although the London jewellers had some success with opaline paste made at Uttoxeter.

Since in both England and France paste was bought by the most fashionable clients as well as those of modest means, it was made up into the lightest and most elegant jewels, not being limited to the more utilitarian buckles and buttons. The Baronne d'Oberkirch said her husband was furious when she mislaid a paste diamond bracelet clasp for not only was it a family piece, but it was much admired on account of the elegant setting. Prices were reasonable: in 1736 a pair of paste buckles cost 2 guineas and in 1752 a pair of three drop paste earrings, 4 guineas. Regional crystals such as Bristowes mined near Bristol were set in women's belt buckles, and Roderick Random in the novel by Tobias Smollett (1748) wore them in his shoes and breeches buckles. Marcasite was widely used in Switzerland where diamonds were forbidden, and cut into small stones and facetted it embellished blue and red glass plaques, imitating the diamond-set enamels which only the rich could afford. From the 1760s it was combined with cut steel, the manufacture of which was developed by Mathew Boulton at his works in Soho, Birmingham, and exported to Europe for chatelaines, pendants, bracelets, brooches, earrings, dress combs, watch keys and buttons. Cut steel was also used with enamels from Staffordshire and ceramics, particularly plaques depicting the fabulous history of the Greeks and Romans made by Josiah Wedgwood, and the matt surface of the jasper combined well with the burnished metal. Equally attractive to Neo Classical taste were the glass reproductions of ancient and modern cameos and intaglios, advertised from 1775 by James Tassie: 'the ladies will not only find a very great variety of intaglios for seals, but cameos for pendants and bracelets of execution sufficient to gratify the delicacy of their taste.'[7] Pearls were imitated in wax, and a cheap variety was *coque de perle* from the periwinkle, not the oyster; freshwater pearls from Scotland and Ireland were used for earrings, if not too grey.

Semi-precious stones, such as cornelian, liked for its blood-red colour, were made into suites, and moss

22 *Gold commemorative pendant, c. 1785. The hair of the person commemorated has been used for the branches of the weeping willow, with the cipher inscribed on a plinth supporting a symbolic urn.*

agate was prized on account of the inclusions which adventitiously represented trees, landscapes and even figurative scenes. It was often framed with garnets, which according to the *Lady's Magazine* of 1798, were the most popular stones for daytime jewellery, and in Oliver Goldsmith's play, *She Stoops to Conquer*

*23 Cut steel and Wedgwood belt buckle, c. 1780.
The matt surface of the Wedgwood jasper harmonizes
well with the metallic frame and the subject — Maria
mourning her lover — is taken from the novel by
Laurence Sterne, and not from classical myth and
history.*

(1773) Mrs Hardcastle declares them 'the most becoming things in the world to show off a clear complexion.' The Dowager Princess of Wales was fond of them too and the sale held by Christies in 1773 after her death in 1772 included several garnet suites. The best stones were imported from Hungary to Venice, Cremona and Ferrara where they were so well worked that when foiled they were mistaken for rubies. Flat, thinly cut and well polished, set in silver gilt, foiling transformed them into an attractive rose red. Similar glowing colour effects were obtained from amber from the Low Countries which was also set in silver over red foil.

The memorial jewellery which was already an important category in the seventeenth century became immensely fashionable after the publication of the novel by J.J. Rousseau, *La Nouvelle Héloïse* (1761) exalting sentiment and virtue in contrast to the artificiality of the world of the salon and court. Hair was plaited or worked into mesh-like patterns and incorporated into brooches, clasps and pendants of Neo Classical design, shuttle-shaped and rimmed with pearls, diamonds, little amethysts and pastes. Sometimes a smooth crystal covered a whole landscape executed in hair, or emblems such as a funerary urn or weeping willow. Besides hair devices, ciphers executed in gold, pearls or diamonds were also worn as mementoes of beloved parents, children, friends and spouses, living or dead. The miniature portrait combined with cipher and lock of hair framed in pearls, brilliants or in an enamelled border, hung from a chain at the neck or waist or was set as a bracelet clasp. Men wore them as well as women, and the Prince de Ligne, killed fighting the French in 1792, bequeathed his daughter the miniature of her mother which he wore on a gold chain round his neck, the snap inscribed 'CES LIENS ME SONT CHERS.'

Another novel which impressed public imagination was Laurence Sterne's *The Sentimental Journey* (1768) and the heroine Maria, forlornly seated under a weeping willow with her favourite dog Silvio, was the subject of Wedgwood medallions set into belt clasps and shoe buckles.

The motifs symbolizing the love between men and women — hymeneal torches, turtle doves, myrtle leaves, interlaced hearts, lovers' crowns, padlocks, arrows and Cupid in various disguises — already in the vocabulary of Rococo jewellery, remained in that of the Neo Classical period. Besides ciphers and personal monograms whole mottoes, most of them sentimental, such as 'AMITIE', were spelt out in rose diamonds. Queen Charlotte of England owned an emerald heart set transparent, framed in brilliants and

24 Enamelled and paste plaque, second half of eighteenth century. Amorous motifs, such as the dove on the altar of love shown here, and hearts, Cupid's arrows and torches are a feature of both Rococo and Neo Classical jewellery.

pierced by a diamond arrow with festoon attached enclosing the diamond motto 'AMICITIA AETERNA'.

Marie Leczinska, Queen of Louis XV, once remarked that whereas a man was judged by what was inside his head, with women it was what they wore in their hair which counted, and the headdress was certainly the high point of eighteenth-century elegance. Natural flowers, feathers and ribbons were pinned with diamond brooches and necklaces of pearls or diamonds were arranged in festoons on snow-white powdered heads together with aigrettes worn to one side. The early designs of flowers and leaves were bent under the weight of pearls and drop-shaped stones, such as the wedding gift of the Prince of Orange to his English bride in 1733 — a green diamond of vast size, the shape of a pear, and two prodigiously large pearls which were fastened to wires and hung loose on her hair. Such jewels were called 'pioggia'

meaning a flood or downpour, and showered on the coiffure underlining each movement of the head. Large stones lent themselves well to this type of jewel, and Madame de Pompadour reserved a great topaz weighing 39½ carats for her hair. When the Comtesse du Nord attended the theatre of the Petit Trianon with a little bird in her hair standing on a rose and set on springs so that his outstretched wings shimmered throughout the performance, no-one could look at her, so brilliant was the blaze of diamonds. Another Neo Classical fashion was to make the head resemble the twinkling of the heavens and the *Lady's Magazine*

25 Silver and diamond ornaments for the hair and dress, second half of the eighteenth century. Light and naturalistic, these ornaments would give sparkle and importance to full dress toilettes.

*26 Designs for rings, brooches, necklace and earrings,
c. 1780. Elegant Neo Classical austerity represented
by designs of a geometric character: octagons,
pointed ovals and festoons.*

of 1777 illustrated a bandeau painted with the signs
of the zodiac and interspersed with diamond stars to
give this effect. In addition 'poufs de sentiment' —
mementoes of people and items of personal significance were introduced into coiffures which grew ever
higher with the aid of pads and rolls, sometimes combined with other jewels including ribbons of pearls
and diamonds as well as tall swaying feathers.

Before high hairstyles came into fashion those who
owned many diamonds liked to wear them on a cap,
sewn to the binding at the edge to give sparkle to
the face, or arranged in designs of butterflies and
flowers. Topazes and garnets were used in the same
way, set off by the colour of the cap underneath.
Jewellery also gave an extra touch of elegance to the
hats worn by both men and women. The brim of the
cocked hat was buttoned with a cockade in the form
of a jewelled loop enclosing a central stone of some
size, and buckles fastened the bands trimming high-
crowned riding hats. Pouget illustrates delightful hat

jewellery: loops and 'rubans de tete' in diamonds,
'parfait contentements' for the back, 'becs de bonnet'
for the front, as knots and bows, sprigs and miniature
hats.

For 'undress' simple pins were worn in groups as the
Duchess of Northumberland noticed when she visited
Madame du Barry at home: 'she had nothing on her
head but seven diamond pins, a negligée of chintz and
very little gold.'[8] This quantity of pins could be made
up into another jewel such as a cross or necklace, and
such transformations now became a consideration in
jewellery design. In 1758 Mrs Greville reported from
Paris that 'nobody can be dressed without diamond
pins which one must have to the value of a guinea or
£20 — the principal pin must be put in the poke of
the cap and the ribbon, pinned on for those who wear
caps and those who don't stick them in curls or pom-
poms, but diamond pins must appear in the head
"d'une femme accommodée selon le bon ton." '[9]
Designs were usually simple clusters of stones forming
rosettes, and Lady Isabella Bentinck gave her daughter
Elizabeth on her marriage in 1769 to the Earl of
Tyrone 'a brilliant diamond pin for the poke of the
cap, one middling sized diamond in the middle and
eight small round it.'[10]

*27 Lady Hertford, by A. Roslin, c. 1765. The wife
of the English ambassador to Paris (1763-5) is dressed
in the French fashion with pendant earrings, pearls
at the throat, a diamond bow necklet with slide and
cross pendant, and a set of graduated stomacher
brooches.*

Since the ears were left showing whether the hair
was dressed high or flat, earrings were almost as indis-
pensable as clothing, in spite of the ordeal of piercing
which had to be endured. Formal designs were influenced by hairstyles, but for day simple snaps were the
rule, as Samuel Richardson describes Clarissa Harlowe
(1747-8) in his novel: 'her headdress a Brussels lace

mob, pale primrose morning gown, embroidered cuffs and a pair of diamond snaps in her ears and neat buckles in her shoes.' These snaps or clips were set with stones in clusters – seed pearls, moss agate, or paste. Being worn so close to the face, earrings were often sold *en suite* with the brooches, bows and crosses worn at the neckline. Lady Jane Coke in 1749 paid £3 for a pair of shell pearl earrings with matching cross, and in 1750 she bought for a friend a pair of Scots pebble earrings also with cross, 'they are extremely the fashion and very pretty'.[11] The Dowager Princess of Wales had 'undress' earrings of amethysts and brilliants and another pair with large jacinths framed in brilliants with matching bow. Marcasite and paste were cheap and popular, and for mourning were combined with jet.

Earrings were adaptable and could be diminished or enlarged as the occasion required. Top clusters could be converted to evening wear with the addition of pendants as Miss Sterling in the play, *The Clandestine Marriage* (1766) explained: 'What d'ye think of . . . this pair of earrings set transparent? Here the tops you see will take off the morning in an undress.'[12] Open settings which let the light through the front and back of the stones flattered and lit up the face. Small round snaps with single pendants of pearls and diamonds suited the simple, loose-waved hair of the first half of the eighteenth century, but as the hair was dressed higher, and more and more jewels were pinned in it, earrings became longer too. Designs were conservative, being based on the bow and girandole fashion of Louis XIV, the drops fixed to the top by a bow and framed in diamonds. During the reign of Louis XVI 'pendeloque' styles were introduced with one pendant only, but sometimes 2-3 in. (5-8 mm) long, attached to a simple cluster.

Neck ornaments were mounted on flat velvet ribbons encircling the throat, or hung from silk or cord attached to ruffles of different designs and materials. Lady Jane Coke sent a cross to her friend Mrs Eyre of Derby and assured her 'you can't mistake putting the ribbon to it and as to length you may either wear the cross upon your neck or the bottom to it to touch the top of your stays. I am very glad Mr Russell acquitted himself so well, he certainly sets neater than anybody – when you have your cross, earrings and roses you will be well dressed enough for an installation [Garter ceremony at Windsor].' Full-dress crosses tended to be simplified arrangements of fine stones – that of the Queen of Spain was valued at the huge sum of two millions – but Rococo taste softened the severe outlines by entwining ribbons round the arms. Bows were worn at the neck and also

hearts; Madame du Barry ordered one of these set with a yellow diamond from the jeweller Leblanc.

In the first half of this period the stomacher brooch embellishing the upper part of the dress was best shown without the competition of jewels at the throat but soon after mid-century the necklace and neckband returned to favour for both day and formal wear. The 'neat pearl and garnet chain necklace with fall and cross and pair of undress earrings to suit' sold after the death of the Dowager Princess of Wales, exemplifies the former, while grand occasions required diamonds. Queen Marie Leczinska wore the Regent in the centre of a band of diamonds on velvet, the stones glittering against the black ground, and this style was adopted in England by Mrs Spencer, whose husband had inherited the Duchess of Marlborough's jewellery. The resplendent effect of a single row of diamonds was admired and high fashion around 1776, though the necklaces published by Pouget composed of bows or loops of ribbons enclosing flowerheads were also worn in the Louis XVI period, together with festoon designs.

Although eclipsed by the diamond ever since the first decades of the century pearls continued to play their part in the toilette, being made up into single rows, twisted into torsades, mixed with diamonds into broad chokers, or in arrangements of bows and festoons tied at the back with ribbons. While visiting the Low Countries in the suite of the Comte and Comtesse du Nord the Baronne d'Oberkirch admired the pearls of the Archduchess, considered the most beautiful in the whole of Europe, and commented

28 Silver and diamond stomacher brooch, c. 1750. The elaborate ribbonwork design is an eighteenth-century interpretation of the seventeenth-century Sevigné.

that they were so much more becoming to the skin than diamonds; she added that this was what the clever women of the court of Louis XIV understood so well, never appearing in anything else. For daytime wear, long chains of imitation pearls were slung baldric-wise across the shoulder, sometimes mixed with cornelians or coloured beads, and hung with a medallion or miniature at the waist.

The stomacher brooch was as important an item in costume as before, and up to mid-century the emphasis was on size, exemplified by the huge floral spray

30   Designs for sleeve brooches by J.H. Pouget, 1762. ▷
These compact compositions of flowers and leaves in baskets or sprays tied in ribbons were made up in paste as well as precious stones.

filling the space between neckline and waist worn by Clementina Sobieska in her portrait. Floral compositions were a speciality of the French jeweller Lempereur, and they delighted owners such as Miss Sterling in *The Clandestine Marriage*: 'I have a bouquet to come home to tomorrow, made up of diamonds, rubies, emeralds, topazes and amethysts, jewels of all colours – red, green, blue and yellow intermixed, the prettiest thing you ever saw.' Half a dozen or more flowers or leaves might be combined together and placed to the side of the neckline, or in front of the bodice as a

29   Clementina Sobieska Stuart (1702-35), School of Rome, c. 1719. She wears a single jewel above the forehead, ropes of pearls looped at the shoulder, and a stomacher of jewelled and enamelled flowers.

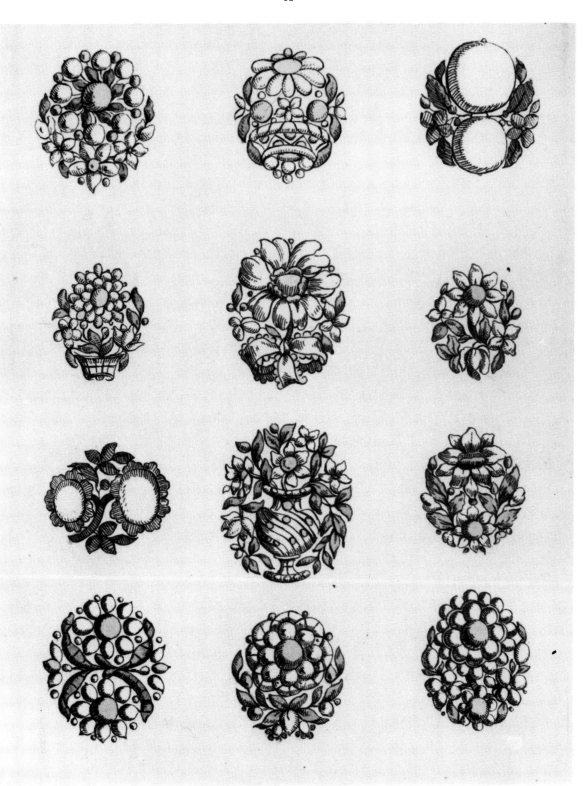

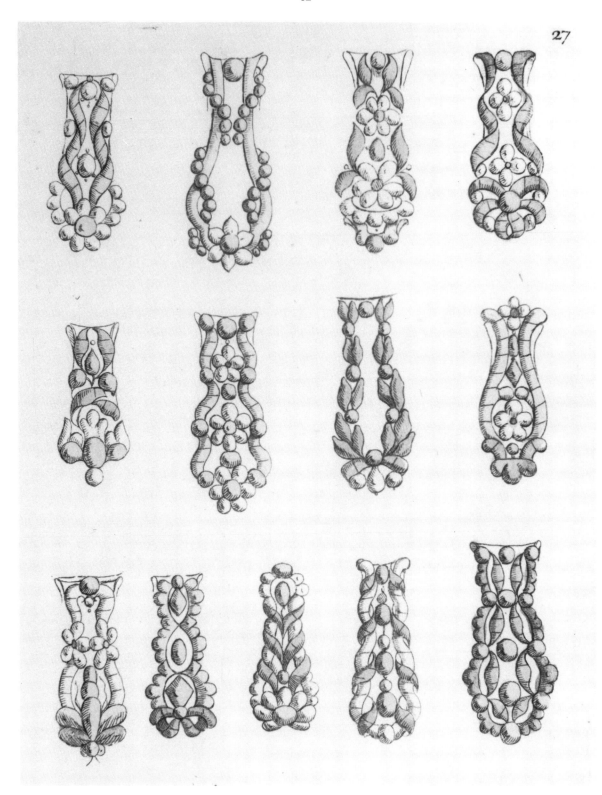

stomacher. Marie Antoinette did not wear stomachers of large size, but liked jewelled flowers, ordering a bouquet of wild roses and hawthorns from Bapst in 1788. In the course of the century the Sevigné was transformed into a light openwork jewel, composed of loops simulating floral patterned silk, and was made in sets of graduated size rather than a single large ornament. Jewellers achieved marvels of elaboration with ribbonwork and flowers combined into single symmetrical compositions.

Smaller dress brooches flashed light and spots of concentrated colour from shoulders, bodice and skirt. The Russian Crown jewels included bows and tassels for the shoulders, wide borders of diamond lace trimmings and a set of 46 openwork diamond leaves, now in the Victoria and Albert Museum. These buckles, buttons and pins for clasping the sleeves, fastening the stays, holding up the train and keeping the panier hoops in place are illustrated by Pouget and are almost all floral in style — loops of ribbon and flowerheads, round brooches of flowers in baskets. The edges of the fichu were joined together by jewelled pins and the commonest designs — clusters, six-petalled flowers, cable and anchors — gave way in the last decades to highly personal jewels of sentiment — shuttle shapes rimmed with pearls or little amethysts enclosing hair devices. As an alternative, and also for pinning cravats and jabots, Wedgwood plaques of ancient philosophers, poets, orators, gods and goddesses set in gold or pinchbeck were worn by those with classical tastes, as were the larger medallions in cut steel surrounds to fasten the sash at the waist.

Wedgwood also manufactured buttons which he advertised as worn by the nobility in different parts of Europe. The decorative emphasis of men's clothes was now placed more on clothes than on jewellery; at the beginning of the period garments were lavishly embroidered or woven or trimmed with metal threads, but as they became plainer they were relieved by buttons of a decorative quality in matching sets of large size. Buckles were important accessories too, a man's social status being assessed by the quality of his shoe and breeches buckles. Giving the final touch of elegance to the leg, shoe buckles were as rich as the owner could afford and increasingly large until they disappeared in the 1790s. Jewelled insignia of superlative quality adorned kings, ministers and ambassadors on full dress occasions, and the collection of the Electors of Saxony, considered the most splendid in Europe, can be seen today in the Grünes Gewölbe of Dresden. The man about town who belonged to no Order of Chivalry made do with quantities of rings, seals and diamond pins.

Bracelets emerging from the soft ruffles, ruches and frilled sleeves were worn all the time, but were conservative in design, the bands being strung with rows of pearls, or made of wide plaits of hair or silk or velvet. It was the clasps which offered scope for originality and by day the most popular were sentimental in character, enclosing hair devices, miniatures or ciphers and usually worn in pairs. Miss Sterling (*The Clandestine Marriage*) asks 'What d'ye think of these bracelets? I shall have a miniature of my father set round with diamonds to one and Sir John's to the other'. The frames of the clasps were decorated with trophies of military, musical and gardening themes, and some with amorous symbols — billing doves, twinned hearts, or pilgrims' emblems referring to the journey to the island of love: shells, flasks, staff and purse. The inventory of Madame de Pompadour's jewellery lists many beautiful bracelets and some of them have survived, including a pair of clasps set with cameo portraits of Louis XV and his ancestor Henri IV, both framed in wreaths of carved emerald laurel leaves tied with rose diamond ribbons. Pairs of cameo subjects could be obtained cheaply from James Tassie, and from Wedgwood. Cut steel was considered very smart, especially when combined with royal blue enamel to give richness to the burnished metal. These bracelets, like rings, were as carefully chosen as the jewels adorning head and dress; like them they were always elegant, and as expressive of the eighteenth-century civilisation as the paintings of Watteau and the sculpture of Houdon.

3

Richness and Eclecticism
1789-1870

The jewellery of the years of political change and industrial progress which followed the French Revolution of 1789 presents a complex picture in which France continues to dominate. The grandiose style of Napoleon I was subsequently adopted, with modifications, by the Bourbons after 1815, and by other European royalty as well as the British aristocracy, whom the ownership of land and coal had greatly enriched. Beyond this limited clientele was the ever increasing business class for whom jewellery was the means of demonstrating social importance, and whose taste was also for the massive and showy. Since the sober clothing now worn by men left little room for ornament, most jewels were designed for women, and these followed fashions in dress with the distinction between formal and informal wear being maintained and mourning being observed more scrupulously than ever. Sentiment continued to inspire a large category of jewels commemorating friendships, love and marriage, interpreted in a variety of materials from emeralds to human hair. Illustrated magazines such as *La Belle Assemblée* and *The World of Fashion* kept their large readership in touch with changes in styles and to meet demand, methods of mass production were developed; by 1845 as many as 5000 families were making jewellery in Birmingham, divided into 22 specialist traders. Output was further stimulated after the introduction of steam — or gas-powered machinery in the 1860s. Inexpensive stones, paste and artificial pearls were set in multiple units stamped by die instead of cast and chased, so that every woman with pretensions to gentility could afford the most up-to-date jewels and trinkets. These were often re-interpretations of jewellery from the medieval and Renaissance periods, following the Romantics in art and literature who reacted against the classical tradition. French leadership in both jewellery and dress was decisively affirmed with the proclamation of Napoleon III as Emperor in 1852, for with his Empress, Eugénie, he made his court the most brilliant in Europe, synonymous with the glory of France.

In this respect he was following in the tradition established by his uncle Napoleon I, who, recognizing the political importance of pomp and display, identified his imperial image with a luxurious form of Neo Classicism which recalled the splendours of Versailles in the reign of Louis XIV rather than the elegance of the Louis XVI period. He was advised by David who recorded the coronation of 1804 in a painting which illustrates the harmony between the gold-embroidered white satin court dresses with red velvet trains and the opulent creations of the jewellers Odiot and Nitot. Hair dressed high *à l'antique* was adorned with tiaras, bandeaux and combs, low necklines were filled with necklaces of several rows, high waists clasped with jewelled medallions, and short sleeves left room for bracelets at the wrists and above the elbow. Classical motifs — Greek fret, honeysuckle ears of wheat, laurel, vine leaves and grapes were created from diamonds and coloured stones, and some jewels were set with engraved gems. Cameos and intaglios illustrating classical myth and history, which had been the insignia of Roman royalty, were chosen by Napoleon for his crown, since he considered himself heir to the Roman imperium. Both his wives, Josephine and her successor Marie Louise, had parures of engraved gems richly bordered with diamonds and pearls, in formal and symmetrical frames. This style, rooted in idelogy, became high fashion, and few saw any incongruity between the dress of a frivolous hostess in transparent classical draperies and a shawl clasped by a Jupiter cameo, 12 Roman Emperors round her neck, and Plato and Socrates hanging from her ears. Hardstone cameos being rare, the majority of women made do with substitutes in shell, lava and the glass and ceramic reproductions of James Tassie and Wedgwood, set in gold and linked together by chains.

Under Bourbon rule in France the classicism of the Empire was transformed into the solid and rich 'Restauration' style. Cameos of Roman Emperors were replaced by portraits of the kings and queens of France, and the Napoleonic eagle and bees by the Royalist lily. Instead of classical art, design was inspired by nature, and aigrettes and diadems for the

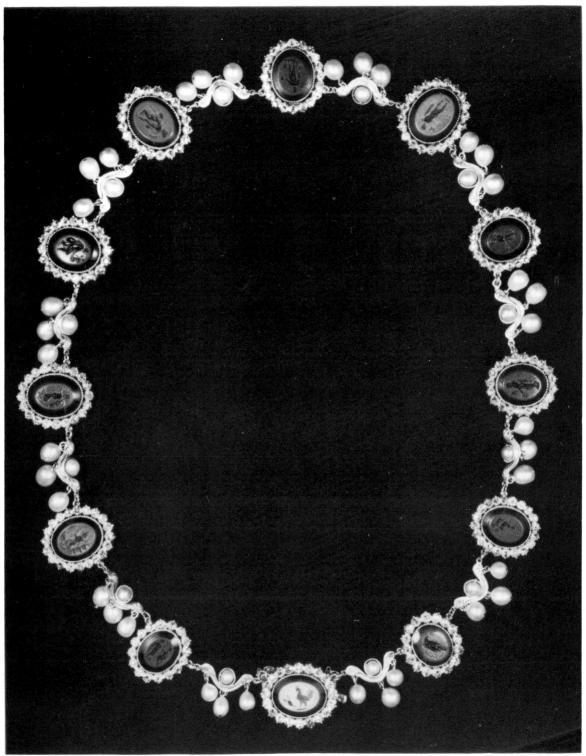

32 Necklace of diamonds, pearls and nicolo intaglios, c. 1800. Genuine classical gems matching in size and quality were rare and reserved for the most important clients. This elegant necklace belonged to the Empress Josephine.

*33 Miniature portrait of a young woman, perhaps
Pauline Borghese, by L.M. Autissier, 1813. En grande
toilette in fur-trimmed crimson velvet coat over a dress
with lace border she wears a parure of diamonds —
diadem, earrings, necklace and belt clasp.*

hair and brooches for the dress were designed as sprays
of fuchsias, cornflowers, lilies of the valley, roses and
ears of wheat, studded with gems, and set transparent
in silver, backed with gold. Parures of necklaces, hair
ornaments, earrings, matching bracelets and belt
buckles of diamonds, coloured stones and pearls also
echoed eighteenth-century forms, but the effect was
different for the stones were larger, the proportions
of the mounts more substantial and the contrasts of
colour and material more striking. Inexpensive but
large stones — violet amethysts, deep red garnets,
olive-green peridots, golden and pink topazes, apple-
green chrysoprases, light blue acquamarines and bright

turquoises were set in round or rectangular mounts
of canetille, or in plaques stamped with stylized plant
motifs, sea shells and scrolls, and joined by chains.
Decorative rather than precious since little gold was
used, they anticipate modern costume jewellery. In
the novel by Mrs Gore, *A Lady of Fashion* (1856),
a character explains why it was necessary to own
several coloured parures: 'I cannot always be sparkling
in diamonds, I must have emeralds for one style of
dress, and sapphires for another — no leader of bon
ton can get on without all sorts and sizes of pretty
gems.' Jewellery therefore was an important part of
the trousseau of every bride, for the busy social life
of the upper classes — lunches, boating parties and
archery contests by day, opera and sometimes several
balls each evening — required a large wardrobe with
the right accessories, and every smart woman wanted
to be admired and talked about.

Count Apponyi of the Hungarian Embassy in Paris
described the Duchess of Dino at a ball in 1849:

> Like a goddess she appeared radiant with beauty
> and happiness, like a ray of silver emerging from a
> blue cloud in her lace covered turquoise blue dress
> trimmed with seven delicate frills, pearl wreath
> and bouquet of flowers for her hair and bodice.
> Besides this magnificent parure she wore a superb
> pearl necklace and bracelets, the clasps of ancient
> onyx framed in diamonds. The ribbon bow at the
> left of her bodice was pinned with a beautiful blue
> enamelled jewel with diamonds and pearls with
> beautiful pear drop pearls hanging from it.[1]

To attain this social triumph the perfectionist Duchess
had spent eight hours in front of her mirror.

The formality of nineteenth-century society
required jewels for the hair, and every great lady wore
a tiara ablaze like a constellation. A majestic innovation dating from the Empire was an openwork tiara
enclosing hanging pearls or briolettes, and other
themes, less grand but very becoming, were garlands
of flowers, wheat ears, crescent moons, Sevigné bows,
sets of stars mounted on black velvet, and feathers.
This fashion was adopted by the favourite of George
IV, Lady Conyngham, for a reception in 1822, when
she appeared with 'a profusion of jewels and a peacock's tail in jewels in her head.' Crescent brooches of

*34 Parure of gold filigree set with pink topazes and ▷
chrysolites, c. 1820. Lightweight filigree settings and
cheap coloured stones of large size created a splendid
effect at relatively little cost.*

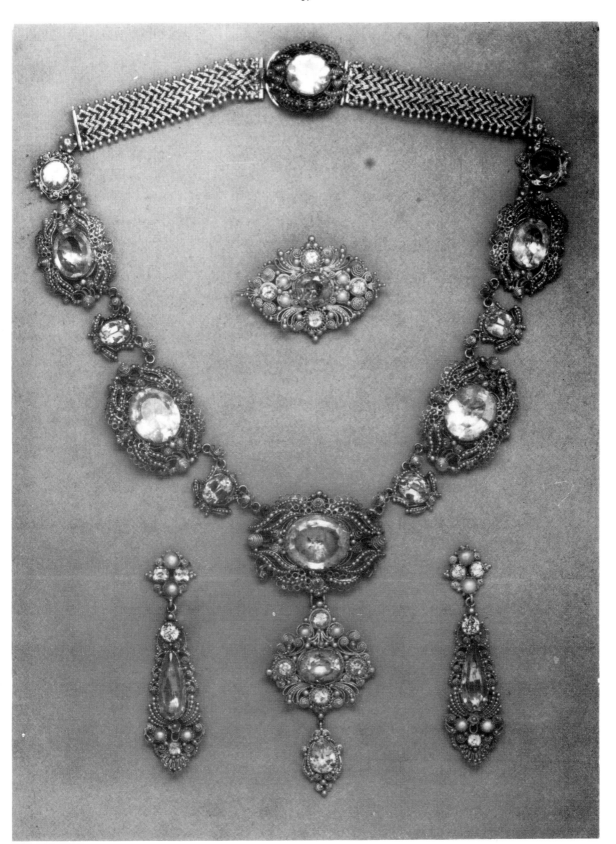

seed pearls were pinned to turbans, and toques bejewelled with feathers and garnitures of diamonds.

Since hair was dressed high, earrings were worn until styles changed in the 1840s. The girandole design of top cluster with three pendant drops, worn in various forms since the seventeenth century, gave way to stalactite pendants up to 2 in. (5 cm) long, or tassels of pearls or precious stones. When earrings reappeared in the 1860s the most popular models were mass produced and advertised — simple tops and drops of hollow gold, sometimes left plain, sometimes pressed all over with a piqué or herringbone pattern.

Earrings were made *en suite* with brooches or pendants for demi-parures worn both by day and in the evening and harmonizing with respectively plain or expensive fabrics. Long pale chalcedony drops with matching Maltese cross entwined with sprays of gold filigree and coloured stones were favourites in England, and other demi-parures consist of long earrings with a brandenbourg-type brooch of lozenge or oval form with curved outlines and three pendant drops. Up until 1850 design stressed the horizontal axis with the oval being placed on its side, but subsequently there was a vertical emphasis and the oval was set upright. Sevignés were worn as stomachers with smaller versions at the shoulder, but not always in pairs, and in 1858 brooches of diamonds or other jewels were fixed on one shoulder, and on the other a band of velvet with flowing ends terminating in jewelled aiguilletes, the brooch often representing a flower in stones of different colours. The strong colours of the stones were further emphasized by contrasts —

turquoise with pearl, cabochon garnet and gold, brilliants and pink topaz, or Royal blue enamel.

Brooches for the dress caught chains falling across the bosom from the shoulders down to the waist, where they terminated in a bright Geneva enamelled watch, a heavy cross, an ornate ring or a smelling bottle. Out of doors chains were long enough to carry a muff, and were made of pearls, coral, piqué, or jet, enamelled, or set with mixtures of coloured stones in gold. Plain gold was plaited, or worked into links of twisted cable, fetter, curb or figures of eight, or else formed of metal stamped by machine into fret or foliate scrolls, or patterned with stars, spots and chevrons. Clasps were always decorative — bobbins with filigree and turquoise, and the mysterious hand of a woman emerging from a cuff, berringed and braceletted.

The list of jewels stolen from the actress Mademoiselle Mars in 1828 is a guide to the best taste of that time, for she was a famous hostess and her house was considered to be one of the most beautiful in Paris.[2] There was a set of eight diamond wheat ears, a rose diamond comb, a jewelled garland for her hair and many pairs of earrings, the most spectacular being bunches of diamond grapes attached to a large brilliant stud. Her stomacher was a pink topaz Sevigné

35 Diamond diadem of wild roses, c. 1840. Naturalistic designs, so popular in the eighteenth century, continued in fashion throughout the nineteenth century.

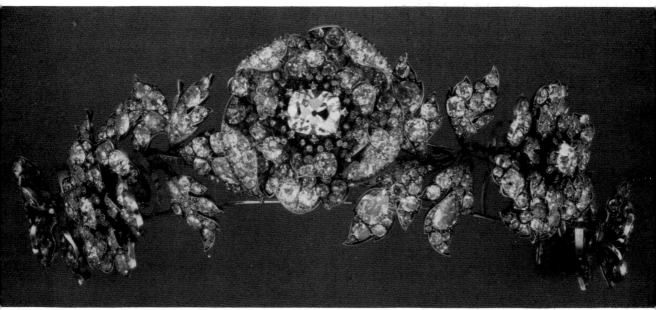

The Countes of Cleueland wife to
Tho: wentworth Earl of Cleueland:

1 Anne Crofts, Countess of Cleveland, by Anthony Van
Dyck, c.1635. The sleeves and front of the blue dress are
clasped with a set of gold and diamond eagles; the waist is
emphasized by a gold chain belt, the neckline with
diamond and gold cluster buttons and a large diamond
and pearl stomacher brooch. She wears a pearl necklace
and ear pendants.

2 Gold and garnet parure, *c.* 1760. The parure consists of
a necklet with a slide and cross hanging from a festoon, an
aigrette, a brooch, and top and drop earrings composed
of flowerheads, leaves, sprigs and wreaths.

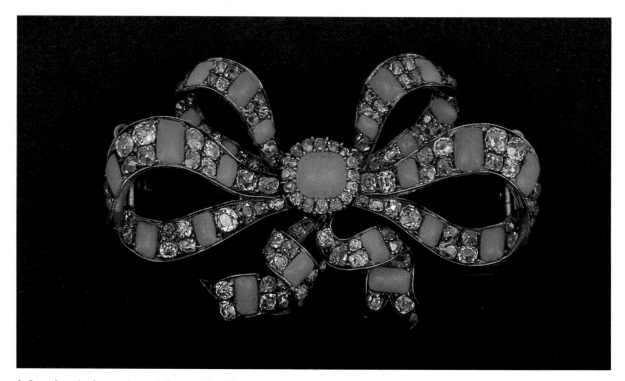

3 One of a pair of turquoise and diamond shoulder
brooches designed as ribbon bows set in gold and silver,
c. 1830. According to family tradition these were given by
the Queen of Belgium to the future Queen Victoria on 30
September 1835.

36 Miniature portrait of a lady, c. 1830. She wears
a demi-parure of long pendant earrings with matching
brooch embellishing the neckline, and a double row
of gold chain.

37 Miniature of a lady, by Thomas Wageman, 1847. She wears a velvet neckband fastened by a small brooch, a large shell cameo in gold setting, a long gold chain and bracelets at each wrist.

framed in diamonds with three hanging opal drops set in gold studded with rubies and pearls, and with it she wore a necklace of many rows of diamonds. For daywear she liked coral necklaces with crosses attached, 'à la Jeannette'. Bracelets were the most numerous item and several were set with cameos and intaglios, including one of gold Greek fret and six turquoise angel heads, and another with a portrait of the Emperor Augustus on the clasp. There were examples of the popular snake bracelet – one in black enamel with turquoise-studded head, and a *bonne foi*, or hands clasped in friendship, gripping a small gold snake chain, symbolic of eternity. Two of her bracelets are described as 'in the Gothic style',

and the belt buckle she had made to wear on stage for her part as a mediaeval princess was much copied, for Romanticism was well established in Paris by this date. The Duchesse de Berri, daughter in law of Charles X, was a great enthusiast, and in 1820 had dressed up as a mediaeval queen for a costume ball given by the banker Baron Greffhule. In 1829 at her own party in the Tuileries all the guests impersonated characters from the court of François II, and as his wife, Mary Stuart, she wore three million francs-worth of Renaissance-style jewels. Entertainments like these, so close in spirit to the novels of Sir Walter Scott, were internationally popular and in 1842 Queen Victoria gave a ball at Buckingham Palace at which she appeared as her mediaeval predecessor, Philippa of Hainault, wife of Edward III.

In this atmosphere clothing and accessories evoking the mediaeval and Renaissance periods flourished so that by 1839 the *World of Fashion* declared that 'the forms of our bijoux are now entirely borrowed from the Middle Ages.' They were not replicas of the rare authentic jewels, but hybrids of both Gothic and Renaissance stylistic elements derived from architecture, sculpture, ceramics, textiles and miniatures, combining religious symbolism, heraldry, trefoils, crockets and arabesques. The outstanding exponent in France was F.D. Froment Meurice (1802-55) a friend of the poet Victor Hugo who called him the 'Benvenuto Cellini of Romanticism'. Like Cellini he created sculptural jewels, but in oxydized silver as well as gold, with figures arranged like actors on a stage. He evoked the concept of courtly love in a plaque depicting a crusader in armour taking leave of his lady, watched by his page holding his plumed helmet, before a traceried window enamelled blue like stained glass. Versions of it were mounted in bracelets and pendants for necklaces, or set into chatelaines as ornamental clasps, attached to the belt. The mediaeval style became so fashionable that a man about town complained that he could not escape kissing a lady's hand without having also to embrace a knight in armour, a page or hound, nor could he raise his head without being greeted by the sardonic gaze of a hideous gargoyle. Derived from the dragons carved on the capitals of Romanesque and Gothic cathedral architecture, these brooches were a speciality of the French firm of Jules Wièse (1818-90). Round brooches set with coloured stones or enamelled were based on the design of rose windows, and crowds gathered round the Duchess of Dino at a ball when she wore a gold belt studded with emeralds and diamonds thus set *en rosace*.

On the Continent and especially in France the

38 Oxydized silver plaque by F.D. Froment Meurice, c. 1840. A knight takes leave of his lady watched by their pages before a stained glass window. This plaque was adopted for necklace pendants and chatelaines.

Catholic revival which accompanied the Romantic movement led to a demand for devotional jewellery. Massive belt buckles enclosed scenes of pilgrims praying at Romanesque shrines, and women carried jewelled Missals and Books of Hours to Mass. Almost everyone wore a cross — Maltese, Greek, Latin or Jerusalem style, in coloured stones such as turquoise or coral contrasting with pearl or diamond necklaces. Replicas were made of the seventh-century garnet cross discovered in the grave of St Cuthbert in Durham Cathedral, and a diamond cross worn by Queen Elizabeth as a young princess in a portrait exhibited in 1857 was copied in enamel and onyx. For men Froment Meurice created an enamelled gold cravat pin of St George — the epitome of knightly chivalry. Rosaries were worn like necklaces, or from the belt, and rosary rings with a cross on the bezel were made in Parma; Archduchess Marie Louise, widow of Napoleon, who lived there, liked to send them to her friends with a request for their prayers.

British craftsmanship compared unfavourably with the work of Froment Meurice and his colleagues, and although motifs such as cusping and trefoils occur, mediaevalizing jewellery is rare. An exception is the

◁ 39 *Diamond openwork Maltese cross, c. 1820. This particular form of cross was widely worn in England, the design being particularly well suited to the display of diamonds.*

40 *Enamelled gold medallion from the Devonshire parure by C.F. Hancock, 1856. The Devonshire parure was set with 88 cameos and intaglios framed in flat medallions enamelled with stylized flowerheads and studded with diamonds. This classical cameo is part of the diadem.*

suite of jewels designed by the architect A.W. Pugin (1818-52) for his third wife, Jane Knill, to wear with her wedding dress in the cathedral he had built at Southwark. He wanted her to look like the ideal mediaeval princess with a chain and cross, two brooches, one of them made as an M for Mary, and a headband copied from those worn by the singing angels in the Ghent altarpiece of Van Eyck, inscribed in 'black letter', 'CHRISTI CRUX EST MEA LUX'. Enamelled blue and green and set with pearls and garnets, ornamented with *fleurs de lys* trefoils and Jerusalem crosses, it was made in Birmingham by the firm of Hardman. It was exhibited at the Crystal Palace in 1851 and Pugin proudly informed Jane that 'no woman not excepting the Queen will have better jewels than you.'[3]

The flat, non-figurative character of Pugin's designs is also repeated in the Holbein pendant, the most typical piece of English Revivalist jewellery, named after the artist who designed for Henry VIII and his court. Adopted as a setting for the Devonshire parure worn by Countess Granville at the coronation of the Tsar Alexander II in 1856, it is an oval medallion with the border enamelled with quatrefoils and hexafoils in bright colours contrasting with a dark ground lightened with brilliants.[4] Many versions were set with cabochon garnets since the deep red stones looked important and Victorian taste admired the substantial and rich.

Figurative Renaissance-style jewellery was made in Paris by Rudolphe, a Dane, and cheaper models in silver gilt and paste by the firm of Schlichtergroll of

41 *Madame Victor Hugo, by Achille Deveria, 1828.* ▷ *The wife of the presiding genius of the Romantic movement in literature wears Renaissance-style dress with a ferronière on the brow. This jewel derived from a portrait in the Louvre entitled La Belle Ferronière of a woman loved by François I and married to a blacksmith.*

42 *Pinchbeck chain, c. 1840. Long lengths of chain were fashionable and were made of cheap alloys and stamped with designs of scrolls, plants, stars and flowers.*

Vienna, so women of relatively modest means might imagine themselves as queens or heroines of sixteenth-century history. Of all the portraits of that period which were examined for jewellery designs none was more influential than the Belle Ferronière, or Blacksmith's Wife, in the Louvre (attributed to Leonardo da Vinci), on account of the pendant jewel over her brow. This gave its name to a 'ferronière' worn at all times of the day, almost as a tribute to Renaissance art, and by quite young girls as well as women. The 13-year old Queen Victoria received topaz and turquoise ferronières as Christmas presents in 1832, and in 1842 Queen Isabella of Spain was introduced to Cortes wearing a double row of pearls like a ferronière as well as her massive arched crown at the back of her head.

Another revival suited to the picturesque clothes of Romanticism was the chatelaine, often enamelled but also made of cut steel, greatly esteemed before the French Revolution and produced again in the periods 1815-30 and 1840-70 by a process in which each facet was stamped *en bloc* into the background rather than individually rivetted. These chatelaines were not to everyone's taste, and the *Illustrated London News* review of the Great Exhibition included this comment: 'here is a specimen of the utmost completeness of those petites affaires de rien without

which the young ladies of the present day fancy they are not properly equipped for the domestic circle. Future generations will stare and blink their eyes when they contemplate the childish decoration of their grandmothers.'[5]

Cheap daytime jewellery often expressed thoughts of love and friendship. There were hearts, shaped into lockets and pendants pavé with turquoises, or brightly enamelled, hanging from bracelets or ribbons round the neck, sometimes with a key and padlock attached. Rings, bracelets and brooches of forget-me-nots, pansies and ivy symbolized remembrance and fidelity, but the most powerful emblem was the snake, which whether single, swallowing its tail, or entwined in pairs and forming a knot, signified the love which outlives the limits of human life. Snakes coiled round the fingers, arms, wrists and neck were either enamelled, studded with gems or left as plain gold coils only

---

43 *Gold bracelet, c. 1840. Twin hands braceletted and berringed hold a snake with a pendant heart-shaped padlock containing hair and inscribed with a monogram. Symbolic of eternity, the snake was a favourite motif in jewellery from the Romantic period to the Edwardian era.*

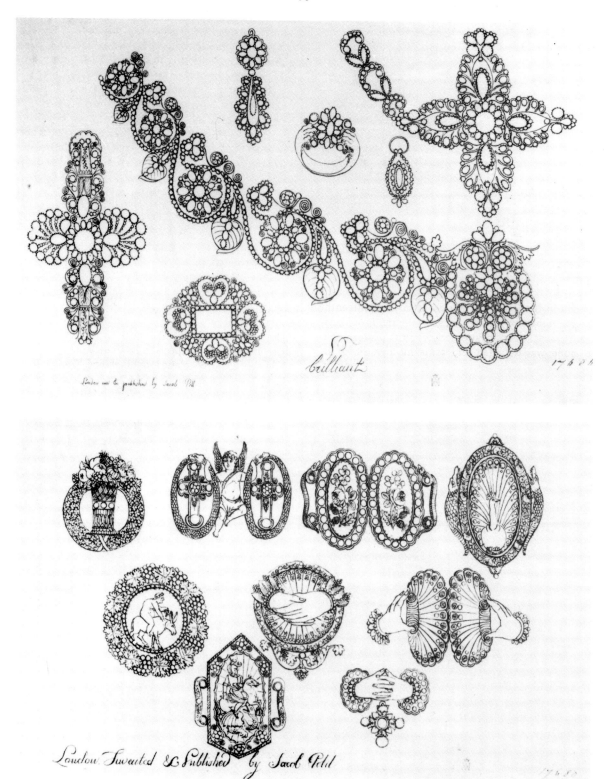

London and be published by Jacob Petit

brilliant

London Invented & Published by Jacob Petit

◁ 44 *Designs by Petit, c. 1840. These represent the fashionable items in jewellery in the middle years of the nineteenth century — rings, crosses, necklaces, belt and bracelet clasps.*

---

the eyes being set with fiery garnets. In 1849 the aesthete John Ruskin was impressed with the appearance of the dancer Taglioni 'dressed in white damask silk, with bouquets of roses down each side, diamond and turquoise comb with roses in her hair. On one arm she wore two serpents, one entirely composed of diamonds with emerald eyes encircling the arm twice, and a turquoise beside it of the same make.'[6] Other emblems of affection, married or maternal love translated into jewels were birds — protecting nests, or offering olive branches, and hands reaching out in friendship or clasped together in token of mutual devotion.

Miniatures of loved ones, living or dead, were worn as much in the Romantic period as in the eighteenth century, either as bracelet clasps or hung in lockets from the neck. As an alternative to the portrait the eye alone was depicted and some mothers liked to have such miniatures of each of their children set in pendants worn hanging from a bracelet. Usually these images were combined with locks of hair which transformed them into reliquaries worn in veneration of popular heroes as well as friends, family and lovers. After the death of Lord Byron in 1824, for instance, his companion, Teresa Giuccoli, sent admirers clippings of hair and samples of his handwriting for setting into lockets. These, made of gold or silver with identifying cipher, were the commonest form of commemorative jewel.

Hair was plaited by specialist firms into daytime bracelets, necklaces and earrings, and even ingeniously worked into landscapes or bouquets — lilies of the valley being composed from the white hairs of old age. The mounts usually contrasted with the colour of the hair, blue enamel and pearl clasps for bracelets of light-coloured tresses, red enamel and diamonds with dark hair. This category of jewels links up with the suites of mourning jewellery made in current styles and fashionable motifs but in black substances such as jet, glass, piqué and onyx. Some were regional specialities, such as the bog oak of Ireland which was also carved into Irish harps and shamrocks; from the foundries of Berlin came iron jewellery, at first made up into classical designs of honeysuckle and fret with moulded replicas of famous cameos used as the clasps of mesh bracelets or linked by thin chains into necklaces. From the 1820s Gothic ornament dominates —

trefoils, quatrefoils, ogival arches and rose windows — and although cheap was worn by all classes of society, the Archduchess Marie Louise of Parma being delighted with the gift of Berlin iron bracelets from her friend the Countess de Greneville in the 1830s.

Berlin iron is one of the many regional jewels which took on a new importance as more people discovered the pleasures of travel, reserved in the eighteenth century for dedicated antiquaries and moneyed aristocrats. At Dieppe the English traveller could find ivory carved finely enough to set into rings and lockets, as well as crosses and chains. Brooches and clasps mounted with Swiss ivory hunting scenes were sold in all the fashionable watering places, as were watches. They were enclosed in cases enamelled with flowers, replicas of famous paintings, and views of lakes and mountain scenery, which during the first part of the nineteenth century reached a peak of excellence. Bracelets and necklaces were made of linked plaques, each enamelled with a young woman in regional costume; every canton had its own individual dress.

The towns of Italy, the goal of almost every tourist, had their own specialities, Venice being noted for glass beads and plaited gold chains, Genoa for filigree. In the centres of Naples, Leghorn and Genoa coral was carved into beads, flowers and foliage, heads of Bacchantes and cherubs, and even into portraits of the leaders of Italian politics — Mazzini, Cavour and Garibaldi. The London firm of Robert Phillips imported this beautiful material and mounted it in gold for jewellery.

In Florence decorative plaques of hardstone depicting butterflies, flowers, fruit and birds were bought from craftsmen trained at the Opificio de Pietre Dure founded by the Medici in the sixteenth century and set into necklaces, lockets, brooches and bracelets. The ancient Roman technique of mosaic work was also applied to jewellery with miniature glass pictures of ancient monuments such as the Colosseum and the Piazza San Pietro framed in blue or red and rimmed in gold for individual items or made up into whole parures. An ancient mosaic of a group of doves drinking from a golden bowl in the Capitoline Museum was a favourite with most tourists, being reproduced many times for brooches. For more romantic tastes there were views of the landscape outside Rome, enlivened with a spaniel or idyllic scenes of peasant life, based on engravings by Bartolomeo Pinelli.

Cameo-cutting, which for centuries had been the Roman art *par excellence*, flourished during the Napoleonic period, and most nineteenth-century travellers continued to patronize the well known

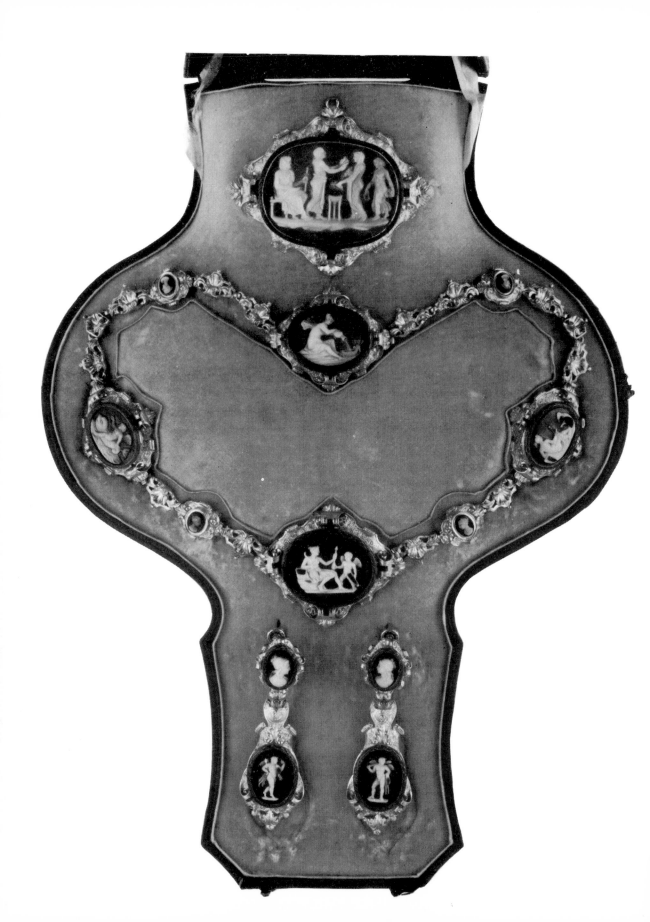

◁ 45 *Parure of gold with cameos. The fashion for cameo jewellery stimulated a revival in gem engraving and these stones illustrate the substantial character of nineteenth-century craftsmanship.*

engravers, Dies and the Saulini family. They sold copies of famous cameos and miniature versions of Renaissance paintings, ancient and modern sculpture including the work of contemporaries such as Canova, Thorwaldsen and John Gibson, R.A., and all these themes could be combined together in necklaces and parures. Besides hardstones – onyx and sardonyx – cheaper substitutes were used, particularly shell which was the usual medium for portraiture. Lava from Vesuvius ranging in colour from olive-green to cream was carved into sets of portraits of great men: artists such as Titian, Michelangelo, Raphael and Correggio, or writers such as Boccaccio, Petrarch and Dante. Bracelets mounted in this way were evidence not only of travel abroad but also of cultivated taste. Cameos were worn throughout this period, settings adapting to changes in style.

From the mid-1850s no stay in Rome was complete without calling in at the shop founded by Fortunato Pio Castellani (1794-1864) in the Palazzo Poli near the Trevi Fountain. There tourists could buy versions of Hellenistic and Roman gold jewellery – necklaces with pendant masks or wine jars, diadems of flowers and leaves. A best seller was a copy of the plaited gold chain from the tomb of an Etruscan princess, excavated at Cervetri by Regolini Galassi, but Castellani did not confine himself to reproductions, although all his jewels were made by the traditional methods of filigree, granulation and enamelling. Completely original designs incorporating ancient coins and engraved gems, and modern mosaics, were suggested by a close friend of the family, the artist and poet Prince Michelangelo Caetani, who also thought of decorating bracelets and brooches with Roman mottoes and quotations from Dante. Inspiration for jewellery came from other periods besides classical – Early Christian, Byzantine, Lombardic, medieval and Renaissance.[7]

Castellani's success was imitated all over Europe. The Campana collection of Greek and Roman jewellery was purchased by Napoleon III in 1862, and provided models for French jewellers to copy, renewing their links once more with the classical tradition. Eugène Fontenay was not content merely to reproduce but took from the creations of the past ideas and motifs which he then restated in modern language. In London the firms of John Brogden, Robert Phillips and Richard Green specialized in archaeological jewellery, which appealed to those who could not afford diamonds yet were too fastidious to want the stereotyped products of the manufacturer: bracelets simulating prisoner's chains, earrings stamped with banal scrolls and shells. By 1862 when the firm of Howell and James advertised jewels described as Etruscan, Cellini, Celtic, Anglo Saxon, Greek, Gothic, Holbein and Alhambresque there could be no doubt that Revivalism was in full swing. Copies of historical

46 *Lady Elgin, by François Gérard, 1803. With the black velvet dress embroidered in gold in the style designed by Isabey for the Empress Josephine, she wears a necklace with jewelled pendant and cameos linked by chains. Referring to this portrait, Lady Elgin wrote to her mother 'it was done by the best painter here and he took unconscious pains about it.'*

47 Mrs George Henry Broughton, by Kate Carr,
exhibited at Grosvenor Gallery 1877. Pre-Raphaelite
portrait of a lady wearing an archaeological-style demi-
parure of earrings and pendant set with silver classical
coins.

Danish jewellery ranging from Celtic torcs and Viking hairpins to the Byzantine cross reliquary from the tomb of the thirteenth-century Queen Dagmar were given to Princess Alexandra when she married the Prince of Wales in 1863.

Besides these reminders of the jewels worn by the long line of princesses from whom she was descended, Princess Alexandra received gifts of great intrinsic value set with quantities of diamonds, coloured stones and pearls. Although made by English jewellers, they echo the styles being worn in Paris where Napoleon III and his Empress encouraged the display of the diamond jewellery at which the French excelled. Suites of coloured stones in the Louis XVI style reappeared for the Empress liked to identify with Marie Antoinette; she revived hoops, as well as other eighteenth-century features of coiffure and dress, and the motifs of bow knot, feathers and flowers. Garlands of diamond roses framing the face fell down past the ears in long sprays to each side, and the masters of this type of botanical jewel, Lemonnier and Fossin, strove to make each bloom as naturalistic as possible, mounting them on springs so that every movement showed them off in a new and beautiful point of view, or terminating them with cascades of diamonds 'en pampilles', like showers of brilliant rain. This brilliant period in the history of French jewellery came to an end with the Second Empire in 1870, and soon after diamonds were arriving in such quantities from South Africa that henceforward the whole character of jewellery was to change.

4

Opulence and Art Nouveau
1870-1914

In spite of the dispersal of the court of Napoleon III and the Empress Eugènie in 1870 the jewellers of the Rue de la Paix and the Palais Royal quickly resumed business under the Third Republic, and some, like Fréderic Boucheron (1830-1902) made fortunes. Besides the wives and daughters of the rich financial and property-owning classes their clients included successful courtesans whose jewellery was much publicized. In England, although the widowed Queen Victoria remained in seclusion for long periods, the Princess of Wales took her place at the head of a society which grew richer every year. The London and Paris jewellers attracted millionaires from both North and South America ready to pay large prices for pieces of exceptional quality, and parures of a magnificence formerly associated with royalty were ordered for the railway and grocery heiresses of New York and Buenos Aires. The plentiful supply and comparative cheapness of the large diamonds mined in South Africa since 1868 coincided with this situation and as a result the number of women wearing jewellery increased, while designs incorporated stones in greater numbers than ever before, often at the expense of taste.

There was a reaction in the last decades of the nineteenth century when some jewellers looked back for inspiration to the delicate designs of the Louis XVI period, and led by René Lalique (1860-1945) the Art Nouveau group turned to an idealistic interpretation of nature, independent of tradition. These two attitudes coexisted during the final phase of brilliant social life which came to an end with the declaration of World War I in 1914. In addition, the orientalizing fashions of Paul Poiret and the brilliant colours of the Russian Ballet influenced jewellery design after 1910.

After 1870 a long period of peace and prosperity combined with low taxation, cheap labour and domestic service provided the background for the women of the upper classes to be permanently on show. They carried the family flag, and a smart wife and daughters were the best advertisement for

a husband's business acumen and *savoir vivre*. The social round of each season required a large wardrobe – dresses and jackets for morning, afternoon gowns for visiting and tea, evening toilettes for dinners, balls, opera and theatre. Each outfit had to have appropriate ornaments, for a certain amount of jewellery was considered necessary even for shopping, and many women would not be seen at any time of the day without a string of pearls as well as brooches and bangles. More jewellery was worn abroad at the casinos and hotels of the foreign watering places of Baden Baden, Ems and Etretat, and at home, for country house visiting where there was dressing up for dinner and dancing. While the distinction between day and evening clothes continued, by 1900 well dressed women were seen with a great deal of jewellery in the daytime as well as at night, a change which Walburga, Lady Paget compared with her youth in the 1840s when 'diamonds were worn only on grand occasions, and it would be considered vulgar to do so in the morning as is the fashion now.'[1]

Around 1895 the display of affluence ascended to a peak, and diamond jewellery was transformed by the substitution of platinum for heavy polished silver and gold settings. Being light and hard, less of this metal was required to secure the stones whose white brilliance merged with colourless mounts which for the first time were hardly visible, broken up by the millegrain technique into a continuous line of tiny 'pearls', contributing countless minute points of reflected light. By this means compositions of hitherto unrealizable richness and elaboration were achieved in settings so fine that the stones seemed fixed in the hair and on the bosom of their own accord, and could be worn with relatively lightweight dress materials. The passion for diamonds eclipsed other stones which

---

48 Madame Cohen d'Anvers, by L. Bonnat, 1891. ▷
The most fashionable portrait painter of the Belle Epoque depicts the taste for opulent diamond and pearl jewellery.

49 Gold necklace with medallions of cloisonné enamel, by Lucien Falize (1838-97). Falize was one of the few who continued to produce gold jewellery in spite of the immense demand for diamonds. He sought inspiration from the East as well as the Renaissance, shown here in the Japanese-style compositions of birds and flowers.

were less frequently seen, and if worn were invariably set off with quantities of brilliants. In 1904, however, peridots were the height of fashion in England, since they were the favourite stone of the king, Edward VII, and the sparkle of diamonds brightened the effect of the lovely translucent green colour. Some women preferred pearls to diamonds, including the American heiress Consuelo Vanderbilt who married the ninth Duke of Marlborough in 1895. Like diamonds, pearls blended well with the black and white colour schemes and soft pastel shades of Edwardian dress.

There was also the retrospective jewellery which suited the rich colours and swagger of daytime clothes of the 1870s and 1880s. The influential Mrs Haweis in the *Art of Beauty* (1878) recommends jewels expressing ideas rather than mere glitter, and she approves of Revivalist styles: 'several of our fashionable jewellers shops contain exquisite facsimiles of old work, so thoughtful in design, so charming in general effect, so eminently for their purpose.' Staying at Broadlands with Mr and Mrs Cowper Temple in 1875 she had written to her mother 'The ladies dress beautifully. Mrs Temple has a dress of crimson plush and rose point lace which is the first lace of all and plain diamonds. But Lady Ashburton wears a plain Keltic necklace of pure gold which I would rather have than diamonds.'[2]

---

50 Orchid comb of ivory and enamelled gold, by René Lalique, c. 1904. Attached to a horn comb, the orchid is carved from ivory with plique à jour *enamelled leaves.*

Ideas came from the jewels of the past on show in museums and exhibitions and a writer in the *Illustrated London News* in January 1899 attributes 'the pretty taste for enamelled jewellery to the New Gallery Exhibition of Italian art a few winters ago.' This exhibition was in 1894 and besides painting and sculpture there was a display of jewellery lent by the Rothschild family. In England the sumptuous recreations of enamelled gold jewels made for Renaissance bankers and popes were a speciality of the firm of Giuliano, and in France of Lucien Falize and Alphonse Fouquet.. Although Castellani in Rome also made mediaevalizing and Neo Renaissance jewels for firm's main business was the production of versions of the filigree and gold ornaments of antiquity, and other specialists in this archaeological style were John Brogden and Robert Phillips in London, and Eugène Fontenay in Paris. Reproductions of eighteenth-century jewellery were advertised in 1913 by Mr MacMichael of 48 South Audley Street: 'marcasite and coloured stones set in blue enamel reproducing the exquisite Louis XIV designs as well as copies of Wedgwood and garnet jewellery — as worn by the old French nobility.'

Far away places as well as the past influenced these designers. Eugène Fontenay incorporated jade looted from the Summer Palace in Peking into his creations, and Lucien Falize who was a great admirer of Japanese art copied cloisonné enamel techniques in medallions and necklaces. There were many enthusiasts for Indian jewellery, and Lord Ronald Gower admired a fellow houseguest at Battle Abbey, Lady Reay: 'an agreeable, handsome and beautifully dressed person in evening dress glittering with the splendid Indian jewellery bought when her husband was Governor of Bombay 1880-5.'[3] Other wives of Indian army officers and administrators shared this taste and also Queen Victoria, whose wedding gifts to her children often included Indian shawls and jewellery. Some of Giuliano's pearl and enamel jewellery recalls Indian styles and colour schemes.

The passion for display which gripped the world in these years can be compared with a similar phenomenon in the late Renaissance and both periods have in common a love of the grandest parures combined with a liking for trivia. These took the form of novelties sold in great numbers at Christmas and illustrated in the catalogues of firms such as E.W. Streeter — monkeys on sticks, chickens just hatched from eggs, good luck symbols such as wishbones and horseshoes. They amused a clientele satisfied with the identical diamond stars, crescents, lizards, beetles, butterflies and hearts perpetually repeated year after year.

Mrs Haweis castigated not only the vulgar glitter of expensive hand-made jewellery but also the debased forms of machine-made ornaments. In reaction, the Aesthetes and William Morris turned to an ideal of craftsmanship independent of historical precedent. For many years the Pre-Raphaelites had worn 'artistic' dress, and with it amber necklaces, polished cabochon stones set in rings and bracelets of unusual design, and their interest in the aesthetics of jewellery rather than its intrinsic value was shared by the followers of Morris who belonged to the Arts and Crafts Movement. The most gifted of them, Henry Wilson, C.R. Ashbee, and Mr and Mrs Arthur Gaskin, made jewels of gold or silver, decorated with enamels and set with a wide choice of inexpensive stones. While their work is highly individualized and easily recognizable, a coarser version of their style was mass-produced in steel and silver; a rather better but still inexpensive range in silver, turquoise and moonstone was marketed under the name of Celtic at Liberty in Regent Street. In France the New Art was mainly destined for an élite, though simplified versions based on its principles of freshness and novelty could be obtained from the shop La Maison Moderne. The guiding spirit was René Lalique, who first revealed his mastery at the Salon of the Champ de Mars in 1895, exhibiting jewels based on the naturalistic forms of flowers, winged insects and the human figure and made from ivory, horn, mother of pearl, enamel in *plique à jour*, or open settings. Gold was the principal element, sometimes treated to harmonize with the enamel and the exotic but inexpensive stones — chrysoprase, opals and amethysts, chosen on account of their transparency and colour rather than cost. There could be no more complete contrast with conventional fine jewellery than the work of Lalique, which placed settings to the fore and virtually disregarded the omnipotent diamond. Lalique made versions of every category of jewel — big striking diadems, collars, combs, bracelets and necklaces for grand occasions, and small brooches, belt buckles, hat pins, chains, rings and pendants for day wear. Much recommended by fashion writers on account of their decorative qualities and reasonable price, each was nonetheless a work of art, and writing in *L'Art et la Mode* in 1902 a critic praised the artistry which invested the most everyday objects with an aristocratic stamp — 'they transform the insignificant pin and the simplest ring into a poem.'[4]

All the leading firms exhibited at the international shows which followed the Great Exhibition of 1851 and those of the 1860s — Vienna in 1873, Philadelphia in 1875, Paris in 1878 and 1888, Chicago in 1893 and St Louis in 1904. They were showcases for the commissions of the very rich and also for the jewellery manufacturers, who were prospering greatly. For the fashion-conscious woman of restricted means almost every design, whether conventional or Art Nouveau in style, could be obtained from the traditional imitators of successful jewellers, the paste manufacturers. The Parisian Diamond Company of London were outstanding in this respect and their advertisements are an accurate guide to current fashions.

Since the installation of gas and electric lighting evening functions were well lit, and diamond ornaments shone forth more brilliantly than ever. Nowhere were they shown to greater advantage than on the head, as diadems resting on top of hair piled high in front and massed into a chignon behind. Blazing from sets of stars, crescent moons and even comets, diamonds were particularly suited to the Imperial Russian sun ray or fringe tiara presented to the Princess of Wales on her 25th wedding anniversary in 1885. The coronation of Edward VII in 1902 gave many aristocratic families the pretext for remodelling heirlooms into new tiaras and the firm of Cartier established in London at that time received 27 commissions, recorded in their albums. These photographs illustrate the variety of design: naturalistic garlands of flowers, leaves, wheat ears, the wings of a dove (emblematic of peace), and bow knots set with diamonds and pearls. There are Neo Classical styles — Greek fret, honeysuckle, ivy and stately laurel wreaths enclosing drop-shaped pearls or briolettes. In some cases tiaras were designed around one stone of particular renown; for instance, the Star of South Africa was the centrepiece of a tiara of dazzling brilliance made for the Countess of Dudley. Specimen stones — pear-shaped pearls, diamonds or emeralds were set at the tips of pinnacles encircling the head, or framed in interlocking loops. Most of them could be converted into necklaces, or divided up into brooches and bracelets, such adaptability requiring skilled design and craftsmanship.

For formal occasions when a tiara might seem too ponderous aigrettes were worn to the side of the head supporting a spray of osprey feathers. Designs emphasize mobility — dove or Mercury wings which could

51 Diamond, sapphire and emerald peacock feather ▷ brooches, c. 1889. Symbolic of majesty, the peacock motif was interpreted, as here, in conventional jewellery and also by Art Nouveau craftsmen in enamels and semi-precious stones.

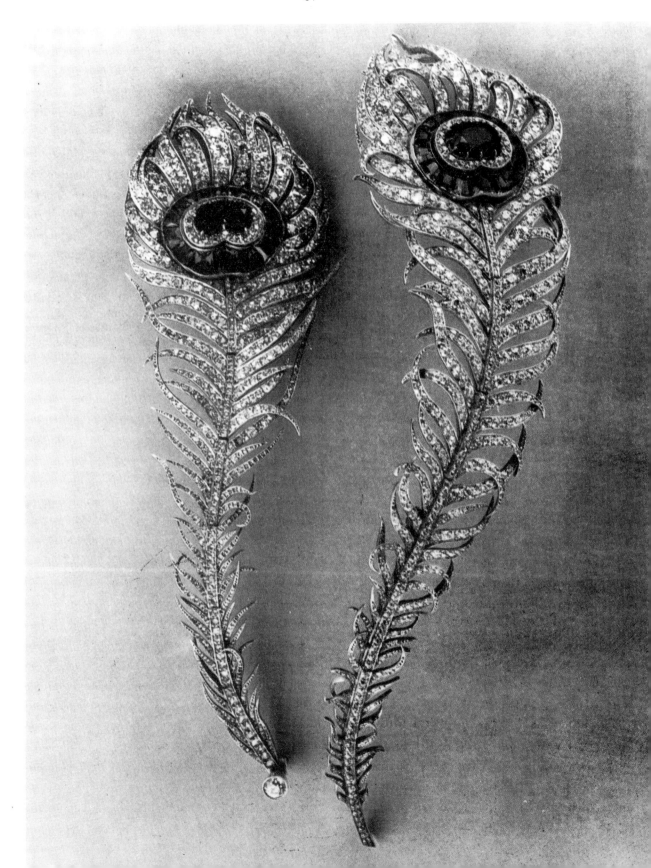

be adjusted to any angle, and flowers mounted on springs which quivered incessantly, casting forth continuous sparkles of light. Always chic, the aigrette was more fashionable than ever after Paul Poiret launched his Eastern look in 1908, as was the youthful bandeau binding the hair close to the face. Combs were essential for the well dressed coiffure and most combined long tortoiseshell teeth with a jewelled heading. Besides expensive diamond butterflies, flowers, scrolls, stars and wings, cheaper materials such as coral and jet were carved into decorative patterns, while jade was considered particularly handsome when worn with masses of red hair. While the Art Nouveau jewellers also created both diadems and aigrettes their greatest successes were in comb design. Lalique's combs were topped with dragonflies, long, pointed swallows' wings, landscapes and clusters of flowers — pansies or anemones, and sycamore seeds with golden insects here and there, all of unusual materials such as horn and obsidian. While the most professional designers such as Henri Vever created Art Nouveau jewels of charm and restraint some of the French were more eccentric as the *Illustrated London News* fashion expert reported from Paris in 1902: 'figures with agonised faces nevertheless beautiful are seen writhing amid flames that encircle them up to the waist or mermaids whose limbs descend into the transparent depths of a mother and pearl sea clasp drowned mariners in their arms. Such a design on the top of a comb in copper coloured gold would appear bizarre to most English tastes, but a handsome French woman I saw wearing the latter in her coiffure with evident satisfaction.'

Pinned to velvet bows, sets of brooches were placed in front of the hair or at the highest point of the chignon. In 1889 the Princess of Wales went to the opera in black, her hair dressed in an original way with diamonds: in the front coil was pinned a large diamond comet and other brilliant ornaments were placed along the middle of the head like a parting, ending with a diamond comb fixed at the back. Motifs for these ornaments were the popular butterflies, flights of swallows, bow knots, sets of stars and pairs of peacock feathers. Such brooches were often given as wedding presents, first worn by the bride to fasten her veil.

Lalique designed hair slides for day wear, usually

in horn, well suited for the purpose on account of its elasticity and light weight; it could be carved into designs full of originality. The out-of-doors toilette was completed by brooches and pins and when in 1886 the Princess of Wales was seen with diamond brooches in her hat many other women adopted the fashion. On 7 May, 1889 she wore 'a diamond bar brooch pinned to the front and a diamond hilted sword pin in the back of a bonnet of black tulle and narrow velvet strings, tied tightly and fixed up against the face being adorned with more diamonds and a pair of very large pearl earrings shimmering against the black velvet.' Hat pins, according to the *Ladies Journal* in 1890, were very fashionable and were 'sometimes of silver, gold or pearl, and very often richly jewelled, others are of cut jet, garnets or oxydised silver, gold Prince of Wales feathers, mother of pearl lined with gold, a Japanese fan of turquoise blue enamel, an ivory figure with spray of frosted gold, a crescent in moonstone with engraved flowers.' As the dimensions of the hat increased, pins had to be made much longer to keep it properly balanced, and were pinned to the left and right of the head, sometimes standing out in space tipped with owls, cats, scarabs and insects in jade, amethyst or turquoise, and as large as 2 in. (5 cm) in length. The colours of the jewels matched the dress; Lady Brooke in 1893 went to a wedding in a violet velvet gown with two splendid turquoise and diamond brooches in her bodice and a turquoise pin fastening her purple velvet bonnet.[5] Lalique's hat pins terminate in sculptured heads swathed in long flowing hair, wasps perched on star scabious, even a group of satyrs seizing a maenad.

Most women felt their dress incomplete without earrings in the 1870s and daytime designs were much influenced by Revivalism: granulated Etruscan hoops, discs set with mosaics, sphinxes, ram's heads, even miniature Roman oil lamps, pierced silver copies of Islamic patterns and carbuncles framed in Holbein medallions. The domed surfaces of carbuncles and amethysts were encrusted with sparkling insects, flowers or stars, and other favourites were gold tassels, Latin or Maltese crosses, fringed crescents, golden spheres and long pendants of jet, coral and piqué. It is in this category that the passion for novelty was given full rein — baskets of fruit and mistletoe, pairs of Willow pattern plates and bells and clogs; there were also sentimental subjects — birds defending their nests, doves offering olive branches. Sporting tastes were expressed in earrings designed as miniature stirrups, saddles, bridles and horseshoes, and even fishing was represented by a pair of gold drop earrings

◁ *52 Lady Curzon, Vice-Reine of India, 1902. She wears a dress of peacock's feathers by Worth of Paris, a diamond diadem and two necklaces, for the Delhi Durbar of 1902.*

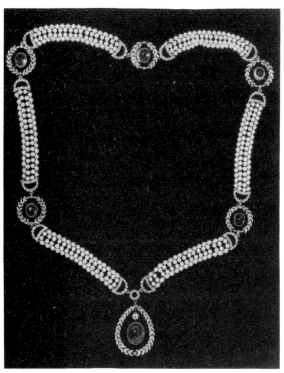

*53 Seed pearl, diamond and pale sapphire sautoir,
c. 1900. This is a de luxe version of the long chains
worn hanging from neck to waist, sometimes with
lorgnette or watch attached.*

formed as trout, enamelled naturalistically and tipped
with pearls. By 1900 taste had settled down to simple
clusters or studs of coloured stones, pearls, or diamonds of various sizes set singly. The complex forms
of previous generations were reset as pendants for
sautoirs and brooches, though owners of fine diamond
earrings never in fact gave them up completely,
keeping them for full dress with tiaras and stomachers
for opera galas. The ever-popular stars were worn in
pairs; also popular were single pear drop pearls hanging from diamond tops and long gold chains of
diamonds, lighting up the face. Poiret's fashions
looked well with pendants, particularly pear drop
pearls, opals, jade and cut crystal. In artistic circles
however, earrings were thought barbaric ornaments,
the idea of piercing was disliked and so there were
few Art Nouveau designs.

Daytime necklaces of gold chains in different
patterns were mass produced and elaborated with
pendants linked by festoons. Some designs are
eclectic – Gwendolen Harleth, the heroine of the

novel by George Eliot, *Daniel Deronda*, (1876) having
lost her money gambling, considers pawning the
Etruscan gold necklace which 'she happened to have
been wearing since her arrival.' Eugène Fontenay was
the master of this type of archaeological jewellery,
designed around pendants enamelled with Pompeian
subjects framed in diamonds hanging from gold chains
interspersed with butterflies. In London Giuliano
excelled at enamelled Renaissance-style necklaces
terminating in pendants. Japanese cloisonné medallions decorated with assymmetrical flowers and leaves
were assembled by Lucien Falize into necklaces
attached to a collar similarly enamelled.

In the 1870s heavy gold lockets hung from short
gold chains or velvet ribbons at the neck, and their
main purpose was to hold sentimental souvenirs – a
lock of hair or a photograph. The front bore a decorative motif contrasting with the gold ground – an
enamelled monogram, pearl or diamond stars, a turquoise horse shoe, or a domed sardonyx. Widely worn,
most were machine-made, the ornament boldly
stamped out in relief. The past was an obvious source
of designs which ranged from the Roman *bulla* and
Egyptian scarab to the Holbein pendant, and jewellers
advertised copies of pendants in the Louvre or the
British Museum. Lucien Falize made a series of
pendants in sixteenth-century style, based on engravings by Etienne Delaune and Hans Collaert. Christian

*54 Reversed crystal intaglio, c. 1880. This may
represent the favourite pet of the wearer, and the
back has a container for hair and an inscription.*

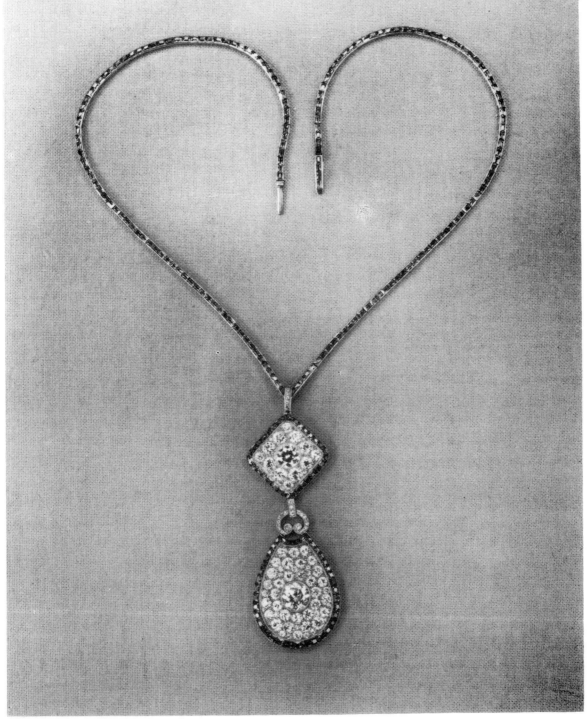

belief in an age of church-going was affirmed by the number of crosses — Greek, Latin, Russian, Celtic and Maltese forms, and emblems such as the Chi-Rho monogram. Cameos were brought up to date. The popular motifs of negresses' heads were 'habillées' with rose diamond necklaces, earrings, aigrettes and hairnets.

55 Sapphire and diamond Lavallière, c. 1900. The lozenge - and pear-shaped pendants, each pavé set with circular-cut diamonds around a large central stone and hanging from a calibré-cut sapphire chain illustrate the excellence of the craftsmanship of this period.

For evening wear lockets worn either from velvet bands or hanging from pearl necklaces were made in the same shapes of conventional ovals, and also stars and hearts, usually densely pavé with pearls, diamonds or coloured stones. Evening necklace design was essentially simple and although Falize experimented and even reconstructed the necklace made for Marie Leczinska, Queen of Louis XV with the Sancy diamond centre, such was the prestige of the diamond that most were happy with a string of graduated stones in plain collets.

Once again the Princess of Wales set the style at the theatre in 1900: 'simply dressed in black mouseline de soie draped over black embroidered jet, long transparent sleeves covered with sparkling embroideries in floral design, a wide diamond collar supported against the throat by a black tulle tie, and a collet necklace of very large stones and a long chain of diamonds falling over the dress, and in the coiffure an aigrette of diamonds with asprey plume and diamond arrow.' Diamond collars were noticed by the *Ladies Treasury* in 1885: 'for the neck nothing but dog collars are seen, these may be of plain or beaded velvet for ordinary mortals while possessors of pearls, diamonds and other gems cover them with real stones.' Cartier mounted festoons of diamond flowers and

leaves in fine platinum settings onto flat and broad velvet bands which not only showed off the elegant design but made the throat look slender. Other innovations were the pear-shaped Lavallière pendant and the 'negligé', with twin specimen stones suspended at unequal lengths from almost invisible platinum chains. The most opulent necklaces were made up into garlands of daisies, roses and ivy leaves or chains and clusters, often with pendants attached.

At the 1873 Vienna Exhibition a black pearl and brilliant necklace attracted the Empress of Austria, but it had already been bought by Sir Richard Wallace, and there was always competition for pearls of quality, which were rarer than diamonds. The pearl dog collar or choker worn high on the throat was another fashion attributed to the Princess of Wales with as many as 19 rows kept parallel by diamond openwork bars, the front emphasized by a jewelled plaque of rococo trellis or flowers, scintillating with diamonds. The size of these panels provided the space for imaginative conceptions and René Lalique made them an Art Nouveau speciality, filling them with women's profiles, landscapes, exotic leaves and flowers, worked 'à jour', and enamelled and delicately studded with coloured stones and brilliants.

The richest women wore their pearls in sautoirs, long loops falling to the waist and caught on the bust with jewelled watches, or as bayardères wound round the neck and twisted into torsades with twin pendant tassels. Small seed pearls were woven into mesh-like chains, and gold and platinum links interspersed with pearls or crystals. Tassels were in tune with Paul Poiret's Eastern styles, but the most characteristic Edwardian pendant was a plaque of platinum and diamonds saw-pierced into lace-like patterns. Chains of jade, malachite, lapis, rose quartz, opals and glass beads from Venice, pink enamel and pearls,

---

56 *Platinum chain with negligé pendant, c. 1900. Like the Lavallière, the negligé was a favourite jewel of the time, but with twin pendants hanging at different lengths. Specimen quality stones were required for prominent display at the neck.*

57 *Platinum and diamond openwork plaque, c. 1900. Medallions of platinum which could be worked as fine as lace were worn at the end of thin chains and the colour of the fabric beneath showed off the diamonds which seemed to hang independently.*

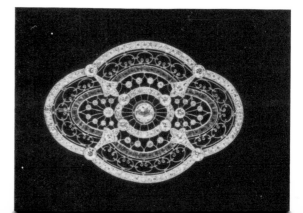

4 Gold, amethyst and diamond chatelaine and watch,
mid-nineteenth century. The Victorian love of richness in
colour and material is combined with sentiment, for the
amethysts and diamonds represent pansies – or thoughts.

5 Stomacher brooch of diamonds framing inlays of turquoise, jade lapis and coral. Exhibited by Boucheron at the Exposition des Arts Decoratifs, Paris, 1925. The striking contrasts of color and material derive from Egyptian jewellery fashionable after the discovery of the tomb of Tutankhamun in 1922, combined with the linearity of Cubism.

6 Platinum, diamond and ruby earrings, c. 1925. The long pendant chandelier design complemented short, shingled hair styles.

58 Platinum and diamond openwork plaque, c. 1900. Plaques worn high on the neck on velvet bands or attached to rows of pearls were also interpreted in Art Nouveau style.

gold links with turquoises in cage settings held muffs or lorgnettes.

These chains were another Art Nouveau speciality, Lalique making them up from links enamelled with plant motifs, the stalks bent decoratively. Not being tied to any given form and hanging free on the dress, the pendants attached to them inspired some of his masterpieces — swans amidst waterlilies, masks with flowers entwined in masses of hair — interpreted in a variety of unusual materials with each delicate and individual creation having its own special chain. At the turn of the century Liberty of London and La Maison Moderne of Paris sold quantities of cheaper versions of this graceful style when demand for long chains and pendants reached its height.

Brooches and stomachers were closely associated with dress, and some for day wear were oval or round like lockets, with coloured stone centres or else decorated with retrospective motifs derived from Egyptian, Islamic or Renaissance art; Scottish and Irish loyalties were expressed in traditional silver forms studded with cairngorms and agates. Almost every cultural and personal interest could be found in Victorian brooch design: lyres and violins for musicians, primroses for keen Conservatives, Diamond Jubilee brooches for admirers of Queen Victoria. Besides the familiar sporting symbols — golf clubs, tennis rackets, game birds, riding crops and fox masks, current models of bicycles and motor cars

were copied. Big game souvenirs were tigers' claws imported from India and mounted in gold, often with earrings *en suite*. Dotted on the dress or blouse and sold in sets of four or sometimes pairs were horizontal gold bars connected by short chains with a small motif in the centre. These motifs could take the form of daisies, anchors and horseshoes, double hearts crowned, or a young lady carved in moonstone, her tiny face framed in an open-fronted 'poke' bonnet filled with tiny diamond points, and a diamond mule saddled and bridled with bright gold. Medallions enamelled with portraits of eighteenth-century beauties encircled in gold rims and crowned with lovers' knots were pinned to the strings of lace bonnets or placed in the folds of a fichu.

At State Balls, Drawing Rooms (when the court foregathered for presentations), and other grand occasions the brooches worn with tiaras and aigrettes were conservative · in design, most often bouquets of flowers which the jeweller tried to present as naturalistically as possible. These 'bijoux modelés' were the speciality of the French — Boucheron, Octave Loeulliard and Massin, and from Paris in 1886 the fashion correspondent of the *Illustrated London News* reported:

the display here is more striking than ever — wriggling snakes of diamond sprays of flowers made long enough to come quite from shoulder to bust down the side of the square opening of the dress — one such in the form of three fully opened convolvuli accompanied by several leaves of natural form and size, the plant arranged as an elegant long spray with the stems held together by a band with floating ends of ribbon — the whole being of diamonds of different sizes set in silver.

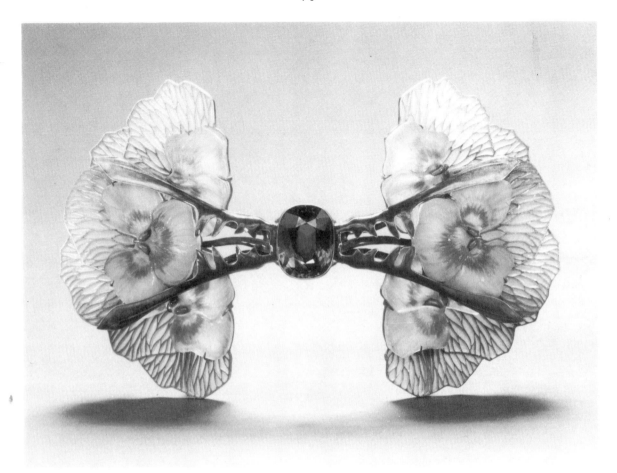

Tiffanys of New York had great success at the 1900 Paris exhibition with one single bloom, an iris, 46 in. (120 cm) long, the petals studded with sapphires graduated in tone as well as size. Another of these botanical *tours de force* belonged to Mrs Cornelius Vanderbilt: a rose the size of a peony entirely pavé with diamonds set in platinum, and valued at one million dollars. An alternative to single flowers or sprays were stomacher brooches of symmetrical scrolls linked by festoons and terminating in tassels of diamond chains. Some smart women liked wearing brooches in sets, nestling in lace and chiffon folds, outlining the shape of the neckline, or pinned to the centres of bows of ribbon. In 1887 at the Drawing Room there was 'a handsome woman in petticoat of primrose tulle over white satin draped with bouquets of primroses and a bodice and train of primrose bouquets, the corsage and top of the train trimmed with large bunches and trails of primroses and two or three big diamond butterflies mixed in'.

The Marchioness of Londonderry liked stars and

59 Pansy brooch by René Lalique, 1903-4. The jewel is made from a sapphire in the midst of two groups of glass pansies with plique à jour enamelled leaves.

appeared at the Duchess of Westminster's ball in 1888 in a 'black tulle dress adorned down the skirt with five large diamond stars and the drapery at the side by a diamond buckle.' Sevigné bow knots which looked as well on the shoulders as on the bodice and skirt were advertised in 1891 as 'copies of the brooches worn by the old French nobility of elegant days' and were like narrow ribbon tied into elegant bows with long ends pendant, some terminating in tassels often sloping off to points, the whole being of fine brilliants. Diamond fringes hanging from shoulder knots and bordering the neckline with a waterfall of diamond chains were perhaps the ultimate in opulent dress jewellery. Certainly Mrs Cornelius Vanderbilt thought hers roused more comment than any other jewel in her magnificent collection. Similar effects were achieved by the diamond lace invented by Massin and exhibited in Paris in 1888. It was made into patterns of roses with scalloped edges imitating traditional designs, so flexible that it could be draped over the dress wherever required. With platinum settings these jewels could be worked almost as fine as thread and the technique was adopted for Directoire-style cravats of diamond lace worn as pendants to necklaces.

Lalique, who dreamed of a total harmony between the woman, the dress and the jewel, complained that few of his clients understood how trimmings on a bodice detracted from the artistry of his pendants; he observed that the delicate and transparent nuances of the glass and enamel were best set off against a plain cream or grey fabric. However, fabulous stomachers are attributed to him: the composition of writhing snakes at the Gulbenkian Museum in Lisbon, women vampires, and panels of crystal winter landscapes of snow-covered firs and bare willow trees. Other subjects of Art Nouveau brooches are dragonflies, butterflies and bouquets of exotic clematis, orchids, poppies, thistles and chrysanthemums.

Both traditional and Art Nouveau jewellers designed buckles and clasps worn at the throat on a lace jabot, pinned to the centre of velvet or tulle bows in the front of the hat, or fixing a belt at the centre. As belts widened buckles became larger and by 1900 no one was considered well dressed without them: 'that up to date ornament which can be applied to a dozen uses in the dress of the day, morning or evening.' Distributing Christmas presents to her staff at Easton Lodge, the Countess of Warwick wore a Doucet dress of delicately painted muslin trimmed with fur and turquoise velvet and spotted over with little diamond buckles, blue sash and picture hat. Staying at Crichel in 1893, she wore a teagown of soft gauze held to the waist by a wide band fastened with an emerald and diamond buckle. Eighteenth-century designs in light rococo scroll and trellis patterns were revived for this purpose, but it was the Art Nouveau school which excelled at belt buckles; they varied in design from the non-figurative Cymric silver and turquoise range sold by Liberty to the floral creations of René Lalique. The blossom itself was treated as naturalistically as possible with regard to colouring, and the leaves were twisted round it to give the outline. Sometimes the

60 *Diamond and sapphire iris brooch by Tiffany, New York, c.1900. The sapphires are graded in size and colour to give naturalism to the design of this splendid ornament.*

stalk was the dominant motif with the flowers — lilies of the valley, sweet peas, hyacinths, clematis or forget-me-nots clustered to one side. The decorative belt buckle emphasizing the small waist was as important an accessory of Edwardian fashion as the long chain or necklace worn over the blouse.

The belt itself was often jewelled — Revivalist types with Neo Renaissance inlaid plaques were made by the craftsman Cortelazzo of Vicenza, and Lucien Falize designed girdles of chased gold. Consuelo Vanderbilt's wedding present from the Duke of Marlborough was a diamond-studded belt, and she also wore her pearl sautoir around the waist.

Hanging from the belt were chatelaines with watches attached and these too were made into jewels to complete a fashionable toilette. In 1886, the Countess of Rosebery shone like the midday sun at a reception given by Oliver Wendell Holmes in a dress of grey satin opening at the left side over a panel of ruby and pink striped satin and finished at the bust with a berthe of ruby velvet — large spray and aigrette of brilliants in her hair, a collet necklace with big pendant headed by a Countess' coronet all in diamonds, a chatelaine at her left side of large stones from which hung a watch, the case completely encrusted with brilliants, and surmounted by another miniature coronet.

While this represented the acme of luxury, more modest examples were always equally decorative since they were placed on the dress so prominently. Watches were made into pretty pendants of spherical, pear or oval shape, in guilloche enamel, sprinkled with rose diamonds.

Bracelets arranged in shining sequence were as popular as ever, the 1896 lady of fashion having 'three or four bangles on either arm showing precious stones of exceeding value besides her neck encircled with chains of pearls, and enamel, turquoise and ruby with fancy running riot in diamond brooches, so jewellers ought to make a fortune this year'. Designs and materials repeat the formula for other ornaments,

61 *Platinum and diamond fringe with shoulder knots and stomacher, c. 1900. Diamonds fringing the neckline in a waterfall of light represent the acme of Belle Epoque opulence in jewellery. This was the gift of the 1st Viscount Hambledon to his wife on the birth of an heir.*

and the massive strap and buckle forms, the imitations of buttoned cuffs in gold, suited plain day clothes as did Revivalist styles: Etruscan beading, ram's head terminals, Roman mosaics, raised Latin mottoes and Neo Renaissance enamels. The most celebrated example of Renaissance enamel was created by Alphonse Fouquet around the miniature of Diane de Poitiers, the favourite of Henri II. Good luck tokens such as horseshoes were popular, and symbols of love and friendship — wreaths of enamelled ivy leaves, twinned hearts, and inscriptions such as SOUVENIR, AMITIE, and AEI (meaning 'always'). Lucien Falize made a speciality of these emblematic and inscribed bracelets. Serpent styles and trellis patterns remained in favour for both day and evening wear, but there was less variety in evening bracelets, which increasingly took the form of gold bands or stiff bangles centred on oval clasps enclosing a cross or rosette. Settings which did not detract from the stones — half hoop designs with pearls or transparent-set gems aligned in rows, either single, double or triple, sometimes varied into the cross-over style or Greek fret, but never obtrusive, since for most people the beauty of the stone sufficed.

Bracelets did not figure significantly in Art Nouveau jewellery, although Sarah Bernhardt's role as Cleopatra inspired one of Alphonse Mucha's spectacular designs — an enamelled gold and opal snake coiled round the arm from the elbow, terminating in a finger ring.

London fashions determined men's jewellery which was worn with discretion, even by a flamboyant character like Oscar Wilde who lectured in America in 1883 in a dark suit relieved only by the solitaire in his shirt front, and a heavy seal dangling from his watch chain. Stick pins kept the folds of the cravat in place, and these were either headed with pearls or gems, plainly set, or worked into motifs reflecting personal interests, sporting emblems being the most popular. For these, reversed crystal intaglios provided colourful representations of game birds, horse's heads including individualized portraits of Derby winners, as well as favourite pets. These crystals were also set into cuff links which after 1870 developed into almost the largest category of men's jewellery; some men had a set for every change of shirt. Up until this time cuff links had been no more than two buttons linked by a simple chain, but now designs included the feline figures of Art Nouveau nymphs chased in gold. Often shirt studs matched cuff links and combinations of opals and rubies, lapis and gold, onyx and diamonds enlivened evening clothes. Snake and signet rings were considered suitable for men, and also watch chains: the latter, formerly massive, were progressively lighter, in a variety of patterns. Seals and mascots (good luck charms such as a pig, or a horseshoe, and little owls symbolic of wisdom) hung from these chains. The most important innovation in men's jewellery was the world's first wrist watch designed by Louis Cartier in 1904 for the Brazilian airman, Alberto Santos Dumont, as a solution to the problem of time keeping with both hands at the controls.

Soon afterwards new influences changed the direction of women's fashion. An alternative to the corsetted, hourglass figure of the Belle Epoque beauty was proposed by Paul Poiret — Irene Castle the dancer, with her slim, straight silhouette, and loose fitting harem-style clothes, hair covered with turban, worn low on the brow and crowned with an aigrette. The brilliance of the colours and the exotic contrasts of the sets and costumes in the Russian Ballet which came to Paris in 1909 made a great impression, and by 1914 Cartier was mixing blue and green stones together for the first time. Both the diamond jewellery in the graceful Louis XVI style and Art Nouveau lost their appeal, and the stage was already set for the emergence of Art Deco.

5

Democratic Luxury
1918-1980

The change in upper-class life after World War I due to the growth of Republican and democratic institutions, high taxation, and the redistribution of wealth brought a different attitude to jewellery, and the couturière Gabrielle Chanel declared that 'it is disgusting to wander round loaded with millions because one is rich: jewellery isn't meant to make you look rich, it is meant to adorn you and that is not the same thing at all.' As a result the heavily encrusted Edwardian stomachers, aigrettes and chokers, the conventional lizards, stars, crescents and bow knots were superseded by accessories more compatible with modern taste. Demand for them was so great that the most successful firms had branches not only in the capitals of Paris, London and New York, but in the resorts of Deauville, Cannes and St Moritz.

Jewels of the period 1918-80 can be divided into three distinct styles. The first period is Art Deco which crystallized in 1925 at the time of the Paris Exposition des Arts Decoratifs. It combined the simplified lines of Bauhaus functionalism and Cubism in light, flat, angular jewels, suited to the shorter skirts, bobbed hair and less rigid distinction between day and evening dress. Colour contrasts were the chief decorative feature – Ballets Russes combinations of coral and lapis, turquoise, jade and amethyst, or black onyx and the white glitter of platinum-set diamonds, which were always being used with restraint. The lead in design came from Cartier, closely followed by Boucheron, Chaumet and Lacloche, but while these three were more concerned with geometrical and structural designs Louis Cartier[1] also incorporated motifs and artefacts from Egyptian, Islamic and Chinese Art, though always subordinating them to the linear context of Art Deco. Facetting and setting were perfected so that almost any outline, however complex, could now be filled with a variety of cuts, and with the 'calibré' technique a mosaic of colour could be built up from gems cut into special shapes of measured neatness, while the deeper tones of carved emeralds and rubies imported from the East added further surface richness. Similarly, elongated

sticks of baguette diamonds, graduated in size, were organized into patterns of white light as the design required. Platinum was almost always used for setting, and on account of its lightness, strength and malleability its presence could be minimized and stones raised high on the surface. seemingly independent of the metal framework.

The culmination came at the 1937 Paris Exhibition when Van Cleef and Arpels, who had always concentrated on giving the maximum emphasis to the light, colour and quality of gemstones, produced invisible settings. Whereas in the usual type of setting, the girdle (the widest point of the stone) is bedded in the channelled passage of a millegrain setting, or caught in the teeth of claws, this process is reversed in invisible setting. The mounter channels the girdle of the stone – a delicate and expensive operation – and inserts half the metal wire of the mount into it, the other half being run into a similar channel in the adjacent stone, laid up close to the first so that although the gems are well secured, no metal can be seen from the top.[2] A further refinement came with the application of invisible settings to the curved surfaces of naturalistic flowers and leaves.

Also in the 1930s, Art Deco broadened into more massive and less static forms with gold increasingly taking over from platinum, and modelled into the thick volutes, straps, buckles and stepped shapes worn with the sportive silhouettes of the early 1940s – padded shoulders, belted waists and short skirts. Since platinum was requisitioned for the war effort in both Axis and Allied zones, gold was the principal element of jewellery made in the years 1940-45.[3]

The success of the 'New Look' of Christian Dior in 1947, bringing back more feminine clothes – long skirts, tiny waists, sloping shoulders – did not entirely exclude elements from pre-war and wartime styles, and the emphasis on size and movement continued. Traditional motifs such as flowers and leaves, feathers, snowflakes, scrolls and loops, formed the basis of conventional and wearable designs composed from mixtures of the most up-to-date cuts of diamond –

the rod-like baguette, the round brilliant, the rectangular emerald cut, the pointed oval navette, the pear shape, each contributing its own particular sparkle to the finished composition. A sense of movement was nearly always present, with diamonds falling downwards in streams or exploding upwards like fireworks. The pre-eminence of the diamond in post-World War II jewellery can be attributed to the De Beers promotion which included the institution in 1954 of Diamonds International Awards, the annual prizes being won by jewellery designs most in tune with contemporary art. A major change in recent years has been the shift away from the specially commissioned jewel to the ready-made, selected from collections advertised in catalogues, resulting in more

stereotyped, less individual pieces. In addition each great house now sells 'Boutique' jewellery, carrying the cachet of their name but at a price which makes it accessible to many. The success of these 'consumer' jewels, and the 'Must' range of Cartier, reflects the desire of women with limited spending power to possess at least the aura of the luxury formerly reserved for the very rich.

Pearls which were so much more expensive than diamonds in 1900 were worn everywhere in the 1920s, both by day and night, in long ropes terminating in tassels, or in shorter rows clasped at intervals with jewelled spacers, and fastened at the back with a snap. Although after 1923 the marketing of cultured pearls by Mikimoto ruined the investment value of real pearls it did not affect fashion. Cultured pearls were advertised as not much dearer than imitations sold by Tecla, and according to Loelia, Duchess of Westminster, it was considered good taste to wear them of a size proportionate to one's income so they should be thought real.[4] Diamanté or paste versions of expensive jewellery were also available, some of excellent quality.

62 *Diamond tiara, c. 1930. Made for the Duchess of Westminster, the baguette-cut diamonds give a modern character to the design which incorporates the two almond-shaped diamonds presented to Queen Charlotte by the Nabob of Arcot in 1801.*

Not many twentieth-century dressmakers seem to have been interested in jewellery, though there are exceptions: Jean Patou occasionally liaised with Van Cleef and Arpels and for a short time Christian Dior engaged Champagnat to design for him, while both Gabrielle Chanel and Elsa Schiaparelli (1890-1972) liked wearing jewels themselves. The latter employed the poet Louis Aragon and his wife Elsa Triolet to design Surrealist necklaces of aspirins, and also Jean Clement, who made jewels of enamelled ivy leaves which 'went like lightning as did the first plexiglass bracelets and earrings. In his spare moments he would invent all kinds of strange machines and gadgets which would light up while we were walking out at night.'[5] Sometime after 1924 Chanel introduced her 'vrais bijoux en toc' costume jewellery of glass beads and mock pearls intended to last no longer than the clothes it partnered. In 1930 Paul Iribe (1883-1935) created a collection of diamond jewellery for her with very light silver settings and flexible rays of tiny diamonds, and after World War II when she reopened the salon in the Rue Cambon, Chanel started the fashion for long gold chains studded with coloured stones. Always elegant in navy blue, white blouse, light stockings, and hung with bracelets and chains which rattled as she moved, with her short hair, youthful figure and vitality, she epitomized the modern career woman.

Social life in England was still comparatively formal; there was a monarchy and court presentations were the rule for every woman of standing. Margaret Whigham, the future Duchess of Argyll, was a debutante in the 1930s when almost every night men in white tie and tails and women bejewelled in full evening dress danced at the receptions and balls held in houses still in private ownership – Londonderry House, Brook House, Holland House, Sunderland House and Warwick House.[6] Tiaras were part of the scene and in 1922 when the Earl of Carnavon gave the family diamond tiara to his daughter in law Catherine Wendell as a wedding present he had it reset as bandeau by Cartier.[7] This style was also the choice of the Duke of Westminster when he commissioned a tiara at the time of his marriage with Loelia Ponsonby in 1930; immensely de luxe, it was designed around the two exquisite almond-shaped brilliants given to Queen Charlotte by the Nabob of Arcot in 1801.

Binding the hair close to the face, bandeaux could be worn flat across the forehead in the style made famous by the tennis champion Suzanne Lenglen, or wound round the head like a ribbon, the method adopted by Mrs Simpson the future Duchess of Windsor, to keep her plumes in place when she was presented at court in 1935. The short hair which made aigrettes and combs obsolete led to a revival of earrings, and screw-type fittings were devised for those who disliked the idea of pierced ears. Design emphasis was on verticality and thanks to light platinum settings, diamonds and coloured stones in abstract patterns or long chains terminating in briolettes or round stones of contrasting colours could be worn without discomfort; they swung like miniature chandeliers, matching the slim symmetry of slinky satin or lamé gowns. The cluster or stud tops were worn separately with day clothes and not only earrings but almost every other jewel was designed on a composite basis. A tiara could be dismantled into six different items: two clips, a brooch, a pair of earrings and the central stone which could be set as a ring. These jigsaw-like compositions were remarkable on both technical and artistic grounds, for each piece had to look as well on its own as when assembled back into the composite jewel.

Earrings reflect contemporary cultural interests. After the discovery of the tomb of Tutankhamun by Howard Carter and the Earl of Carnavon in 1922 the bright colours and symbols of ancient Egypt re-entered the vocabulary of the jeweller, and Cartier mounted glazed faience lotus beads dating from the 20th Dynasty (600 BC) into a pair of diamond and onyx earrings. More decorative motifs were provided by the flowers and dragons of the Far East, and imported jade plaques carved with birds and plants or worked into circles were set into platinum and diamond earrings. In the 1930s, when hair was longer, earclips were worn with tailored town clothes and country tweeds, some in platinum and precious stones, others in gold. Mrs Simpson, for instance, always softened her severe hairstyle with clips at the ears, favourites being sprays of flowers, each minute bloom set with a sapphire, the leaves and stems of diamonds. In 1938 Cartier had a great success with clips of yellow-gold daisies, set with citrines and brown topazes, and gold was the material of forties earrings – pendants with snake-like chains attached, or volute-style clips lightly studded with diamonds and coloured stones. In the post-World War II period the best work tended to be set with diamonds, with neat clips being designed as conventionalized flowers, snowflakes, scrolls and loops with shimmering baguette pendants. Pearl earrings never went out of fashion, being worn in chains and tassels in the 1920s, and later as neat studs, sometimes in pairs of contrasting black and white pearls set round with diamonds. Smart post-war taste in earrings, as in other jewellery, is illustrated

by the collection of Nina Dyer, formerly married to Baron von Thyssen and to Prince Sadruddin, the son of the Aga Khan. Her jewellery was sold by Christies in Geneva in 1969, after her death. The most important items were: platinum earclips each set with a black pearl bordered by spirals of navette diamonds, clips of sapphire flowers encircled by navette and pear-shaped diamond petals, and a pair of Cartier pendants of yellow gold pavé with yellow diamonds hanging

63 *Countess Mountbatten of Burma, c. 1955. The platinum, ruby and diamond earclips are designed as flowers and leaves; she also wears a flower brooch, a pearl necklace and a wrist watch with her day dress.*

64 *Diamond rock crystal and onyx brooch, by Cartier, c. 1925. These versatile openwork brooches could be pinned to hat or dress as required.*

from a looped ribbon top. While by night the pendants dangled glamorously above strapless décolletages, clips were set with stones or enamelled in colours matching the suit or tailored day dress.

Some of the most charming jewels of the inter-war years were pinned to neat, small hats and berets. Loelia Westminster recalled the autumn of 1925 when 'we wore pairs of little diamanté animals in our felt hats, otherwise we pinned real brooches in them which was asking for trouble as they were always falling off or getting stolen in cloakrooms.' Cartier hat brooches follow the same sequence of themes as earrings, the Egyptian Revival being represented by a brooch created round a glazed faience statuette of Isis, and the Far East by carved coral Buddhas and ivory Samurai, all framed in diamonds and platinum. Most in demand was the plain, open-centred oblong or circle, associated with a wide range of motifs and made in many materials: polished onyx with diamond palmettes and rings of frosted crystal held by diamond and onyx ribbands. By the end of the 1930s these geometric styles were being supplanted by more naturalistic designs such as gold bunches of flowers set with coloured stones, advertised by Van Cleef and Arpels in 1939. Although hats were still worn for some years after the War fewer brooches were specifically designed for them, and the floral bird and novelty brooches worn on the dress or lapel looked equally well pinned to the hat.

Necklaces were as much a part of post-1918 dress as in the Edwardian era, and 'sautoirs' of pearls terminating in tassels or jewelled pendants lengthened as skirts shortened, falling in cascades over bare skins revealed by backless dresses. Almost uniform wear, they were the choice of Lorelei, the heroine of the novel by Anita Loos, *Gentlemen Prefer Blondes*, who shopped at Cartier and found 'quite a delightful square cut emerald and quite a long rope of pearls.' Another visitor to Cartier was the art dealer René Gimpel who in 1920 saw 'a long necklace of green beads looping down from her neck rounded off by a green cameo of hard rectangular stone, long earrings, also frame her face,' and concluded that he had witnessed a Renaissance in the art of jewellery.[8] Grooved and carved emeralds from India were combined with pearls into sautoirs and necklaces, and large turquoises, amethysts and acquamarines made up

65 *'Nubienne', by Paul Poiret, as illustrated in ▷ Art, Goût et Beauté, published 1923. At this period numerous bracelets were worn with sleeveless dressses, and long chains cover barebacks and decolletés.*

into colourful chains. Revived by Chanel after 1954, flexible gold chains in a wide range of links have remained in fashion ever since.

Shorter necklaces follow a similar design pattern. Formal fringe and pendant styles are reinterpreted in the contrasting colours and geometric cuts of Art Deco, exemplified by acquamarines alternating with

baguettes. The diamond collars worked into abstract panels tapering behind and swelling out wide and deep in front expressing the rich taste of the 1930s were succeeded by the equally massive but gold necklaces of the forties. These were made from substantial sections of 'gaspipe', 'rat tail', 'snake' and 'mesh' design, the centres sometimes embellished with a bow or spray of flowers with coloured stones setting off the polished metal. This type was adapted to the fashions of the 1950s in flexible gold necklets with detachable jewelled clips in front. Because of the decline in the number of grand and official occasions after 1945 the necklace now took the place of the

66 *Necklace of amethysts and diamonds, and amethyst, diamond and turquoise pendant, c. 1925. The sharp contrast of colour and material — white diamond and purple amethyst — combined with links of rectangles and circles, are characteristic of Art Deco jewellery, and the pendant vase of fruit is another favourite motif which illustrates the same juxtaposition of opaque and transparent, expensive and cheap materials.*

67 *Diamond necklace, Alexander Reza, Paris c. 1960. The slender proportions of the baguette-cut diamond chain emphasize the magnificence of the pear-shaped diamond pendant.*

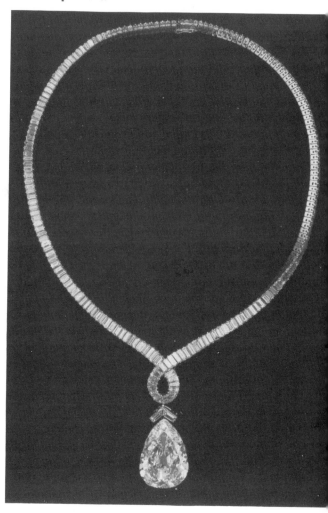

68 *The model wears: a diamond necklace (67),
and ruby and diamond jewellery by Van Cleef and
Arpels — invisibly-set curved earclips, a brooch composed of ten clusters, and a wide cluster bracelet
and ring.*

◁ 69 *Pendant watches by Lacloche (above) and Cartier (below) and a diamond brooch with calibré emeralds and sapphires centred on a cabochon sapphire, also by Cartier, c. 1925.*

---

70 *The models wear (left) a necklace composed of diamonds and cultured pearls mounted as a garland on trembler springs, ruby and diamond bracelet and ring; and (right) sapphire and diamond cluster earrings, a double chain of sapphires and diamonds with three large sapphires in front and a sapphire pendant highlighted by diamond ribbon, twin staircase-style bracelets set with diamonds and sapphires respectively and a yellow diamond ring.*

tiara as the most prestigious personal ornament and investment. The sumptuous evening dresses, 'robes de style', created by the great couture houses required equally splendid parures, and during the 1950s a new style emerged, conservative and sleek. The deep fringes of swaying pendants, the garlands of flowers and the interlaced ribbons always combined several different cuts of diamonds and sometimes contrasts of colour. The essential character of this type of post-War fine jewellery is represented by a diamond necklace composed of rows of round brilliants and baguettes respectively culminating in a fancy-coloured pear drop brilliant – a fortune in magnificently cut stones securely mounted on a flexible and invisible metal framework.

Pendants of a figurative as well as geometric and abstract character were a feature of Art Deco jewellery, close to brooch design. They included plaques of carved jade, figures of Egyptian goddesses, Mughal enamels of hunting scenes and dancing girls – modern eclectic successors to the sentimental lockets and crosses of the Victorians. Bows, bouquets and tassels as well as specimens of topaz or amethysts were sometimes attached to the gold chain work necklaces of the forties. The most significant development in post-War pendants is also eclectic in character, for the Italian firm of Bulgari have revived the ancient Roman cameo or coin pendant, and more recently the ceramic plaques made by Wedgwood in the eighteenth century.

Brooches presented the Art Deco jeweller with a challenge since although they were still as much a part of dress as the Edwardian stomacher, design had to be in tune with the very different world of Picasso, Braque and Gris. Boucheron succeeded in bringing the stomacher up to date with a piece shown at the Exposition of 1925, organized round the interplay of circles and straight lines, and encrusted with lapis, coral, jade, turquoise and onyx within borders of tiny diamonds, recalling the bright inlays of Tutankhamun's pectoral. Design was not restricted to abstract and linear forms and some jewellers used

---

71 Diamond, platinum and onyx bracelet, by Cartier. The panther motif, also interpreted in rings and brooches is one of Cartier's greatest successes.

the surface of the brooch as an artist's canvas to illustrate different aspects of contemporary life. The Egyptian Revival was exemplified by a glazed faience temple portico, and Mughal miniatures inspired compositions of veiled women musicians. Nature provided animal themes of which the most outstanding was the Cartier panther with diamond coat spotted with onyx and gleaming navette emerald eyes. The brilliant plumage of birds suggested other striking colour contrasts, as did flower gardens. Very stylized in the 1920s, the flowerpot brooch developed into the more naturalistic sprays of the late 1930s and these were a speciality of Van Cleef and Arpels, the invisibly-set petals executed in rubies or sapphires. Although openwork platinum and white gold plaques, pavé set with diamonds in abstract patterns, were fashionable throughout the 1930s, figurative designs in brooches continued. The English weather was the subject of a brooch exhibited in 1935 at the London Exhibition of British Industrial Art, the rain falling in baguette showers from clouds of brilliants on to agate and onyx umbrellas. Sport was a favourite theme for daytime jewellery – crossed tennis rackets, polo sticks, skis, sailing boats and racehorses, successful owners sometimes commemorating wins with jewels decorated with their own colours. Equally personal in character were the jewelled regimental, airforce and naval badges, monograms and birth signs; Schiaparelli commissioned Cartier to make her birth sign, the Great Bear constellation, into a brooch.

Brooches of the 1940s and 1950s continued in the style set by the Cartier citrine and topaz daisy of 1938, with floral sprays of light-coloured stones set in gold drawn into spirals or twisted wire. Long-backed birds sitting on golden boughs succeeded the stylized Art Deco models, and were worn pinned in the hat or lapel with a single row of pearls and stud earrings, with daytime clothes. An invention for daytime wear dating from the 1920s was the sureté pin, with fixed decorative motif at its head and another removable, but not always identical, motif at the point, preventing it from slipping out once skewered through the clothing. While the arrow was a most appropriate and popular theme, alternatives were monograms, and sporting and eclectic motifs such as lotus buds, papyrus and palmettes, worked in both cheap and expensive materials. Equally functional though less decorative was the bar brooch set with calibre-cut stones and used to fasten the belt, flowers and scarves. For evening wear, butterfly, dragonfly, feather, shell and fan brooches worked in diamonds, pearls and coloured stones looked magnificent with the soft black silks of New Look cocktail dresses, or pinned to the chiffon folds or low necklines of strapless evening gowns.

Closely related to dress, and purely ornamental, were clips, worn either in matching pairs, or combined into one big brooch, gripping the edge of the fabric rather than transfixing it with a pin. According to Loelia Westminster, by the end of the 1920s 'it was essential to possess a pair of diamond or diamanté clips not only for hats but for everything else even to the small of the back where they served to keep underclothes out of sight.' For evening wear they could be clipped on to the shoulders or along the neckline, side by side, or embellishing opposite ends, and *Vogue* magazine in October 1935 reported how 'a woman client turned down a Molyneux black dress for another with far less exciting neckline because she possesses two magnificent Herz diamond and crystal clips that wanted no interference.'[9] Clips were equally suited to the lapels of tailored suits with padded shoulders, and for the hat, while some jewellers placed them as clasps onto gold bangles. Designs developed from the buckle mitre and circular shapes of geometric character in platinum or white gold set with diamonds in abstract patterns, into the massive triangular and stepped forms of the late 1930s, culminating in the wartime heavy gold volutes and scrolls curved like wood shavings studded with diamonds in star settings or calibré rubies and sapphires. Once the New Look was established they went out of fashion, their place being taken by figurative novelty and bird brooches.

The lapel was an important site for the jewellery of the inter-war period, and an alternative to the clip was the fob pendant hanging from a brooch pin which was worn on the rever, or on the shoulder. Displayed so prominently it attracted attention, and inspired highly decorative designs. While some were purely ornamental pendant brooches made in both abstract and figurative styles, their main purpose was to serve as watch cases, such as the dovecote made by the American firm of Udall and Ballou, with the dial concealed behind the jewelled walls.

From the early years of the century Louis Cartier had concerned himself with the wrist watch, which offered the busy modern man and woman a practical and elegant solution to portable timekeeping. Both the dial and the wrist bands in women's watches were decoratively treated, the octagonal, oval, round or rectangular dials being either hidden under hinged covers, or framed in white diamonds. Usually attached to blank silk elastic cord or moiré silk ribbon, the most *de luxe* models were incorporated in the latest style of gold chain or jewelled bracelet.

Bracelets were worn in quantities in the inter-war years for short sleeves left the arms bare, sometimes as far as the shoulder. Loelia Westminster owned 30 glass bracelets in her youth, mixing the colours like a rainbow, and she commented that the most daring girls wore the most bracelets. Flexibility was the design principle, and in the 1920s besides strings of beads, bracelets were composed of supple links and chains of contrasting coloured gemstones, set into abstract patterns like Persian carpets; they became more elaborate and wider in the 1930s. To this period belong the Van Cleef and Arpels invisibly-set bracelets encircling the wrists with sapphire blue and ruby red bands of concentrated colour.

Negro art, which influenced Cubist painting, is also reflected in jewellery, as Rene Gimpel noticed in 1920: 'On her arms over long suede gloves she has slipped two red and two black bracelets, the fashion is for negro art and the shop windows are displaying heavy bracelets made of bone, hers appear to be of tinted ivory.' Even elaborate jewelled floral bracelets were worn in quantities and Michael Arlen must have had this fashion in mind when he described Princess Valeria in his novel *May Fair* (1925): 'Not one among all the flowers in that flaming conservatory were

72 *Diamond and platinum double clip brooch, c. 1935. These could be separated to wear on opposite lapels or at each end of a square neckline, or joined together to make one important brooch for formal occasions.*

73 Bracelet and ring in gold and topaz by Jean Fouquet, 1936.

more beautiful than the flowers of Cartier, Lacloche, Boucheron and Janesich which graced the young lady's slender forearms in the guise of bracelets of diamonds, emeralds, black onyx, pink pearls, all wrought upon platinum in divers tender designs.' A novelty listed in the 1920 Paris sale of the jewels of the French actress Gaby Deslys was elephant's hair tightly corded into a spiral mounted into a gold bracelet with matching ring, and reputed to bring good luck. From about 1935 lucky charms jingling and jangling from bracelets were the acme of smartness, and Cecil Beaton saw Mrs Dudley Ward 'hair snipped into a short shingle, dressed in natty little day suits of checks, possibly adding a huge carnation to her button hole . . . and as she tapped the end of a cigarette on a gold case before lighting it with her briquet the gold wrist chains and bracelets would dangle.'[10] By the 1940s one important bracelet had taken the place of several worn at once, and designs seemed influenced by machinery, composed of chunky gold links resembling bicycle chains or moving staircases, or bands deeply grooved and fluted. This massiveness disappeared from post-War bracelets which were made of sleek ribbons of gold

mesh, plaited tubular chains, or jewelled loops and garlands of flowers enclosing the wrist in a blaze of light and colour. Unlike the bracelets of the past clasps were less significant, though sometimes a detachable clip was set with a specimen stone such as a coloured diamond.

Most jewellers sold decorative belts and buckles. Gaby Deslys wore a belt and clasp made from gold 20-dollar pieces alternating with enamelled links, and Cartier made whole belts from jade plaques. Most attention was usually given to the buckle which could be an ancient Egyptian scarab in modern mount, or a diamond monogram enclosed in a circle. After World War II such belts were made up from links of gold chain, with an embossed central medallion, and entered the category of costume jewellery.

Twentieth-century jewellery has been almost exclusively devoted to the beautification of women, and many items for men disappeared with the tendency to casual dressing which followed World War I. The wrist watch replaced the watch chain, tie pins disappeared with cravats and frock coats, signet rings were thought ostentatious in a democratic world, and only cuff links, waistcoat buttons and shirt studs remained. These mirrored the sequence of styles in women's jewellery, and reflect the same standards of craftsmanship, always adding an individual note to smart dressing.

Notes

CHAPTER 1

1 Raymond Foulché Delbosc, ed., *Madame d'Aulnoy, Travels in Spain*, London 1930, Letter VIII, p. 213.

2 Inventory of Maria Luisa of Orleans 1689, vol. 5269, Registro de Escrituras de D. Francisco Arevalo, Real Bureo Archivo General de Palacio Madrid. Cited by P. Muller, *Jewels in Spain*, New York, 1972.

3 Jacques Ruppert, *Le Costume II, Les Arts Decoratifs*, Paris n.d., p. 56 and pl. XI.

4 Musée de Versailles, illustrated by J. Evans, *History of Jewellery, 1100-1870*, London 1970, pl. 129.

5 Lucy Norton, *First Lady of Versailles*, London 1978, p. 354.

6 Robert de Berghen, *Les Merveilles des Indes Orientales et Occidentales*, Paris 1669.

7 *The Journals of Celia Fiennes*, introduced by John Hillaby, London 1983, p. 267, and footnote 15; p. 320 cites John Evelyn reference, 27 June 1654.

8 S. Anjou, *Marcus Gunter's Designs for Jewellers 1684-1733*, Rohsska Konstae Museum. 1956, p. 43.

9 Olivier Amiel, ed., *Lettres de la Princesse Palatine 1672-1722*, Paris 1981, p. 101.

10 *Souvenirs de Madame de Caylus*, Paris 1908 p. 67.

11 G. Legaré, *Livre des Ouvrages d'Orfevrerie*, 1663.

12 'Le Portrait de Béatrix de Cusance au Musée du Louvre et l'inventaire de ses Joyaux en 1663', in *Académie des Sciences, Belles Lettres et Arts de Besançon, Procés Verbaux et Mémoires*, 1897, p. 128.

13 *Journal du Marquis de Dangeau, Additions du Duc de Saint Simon*, Paris 1857.

14 W.T. Parry, ed., *Letters from Dorothy Osborne to Sir William Temple*, London 1888, p. 135.

15 Bulstrode Whitelocke, ed., *Journal of the Swedish Embassy in the Years 1653-54*, London 1855, p. 202.

16 *Memoirs of Ann, Lady Fanshawe 1600-1672*, London 1907, p. 147.

17 Accession no. M. 143.1975.

18 Exhibition of Gemstones and Jewellery, City of Birmingham Museum and Art Gallery, 1960, no. 307.

19 M.H. Gans, *Juwelen en Mensen*, Amsterdam 1961, plate XIV.

CHAPTER 2

1 Jean Bourguet, *Second Livre de taille d'épargne et de bas relief en émail ou noir d'écaille et ouvrages d'horlogerie*, 1723.

2 Augustin Duflos, *Recueil de desseins de joaillerie fait par Augustin Duflos en XXVIII feuilles remplies de differentes ouvrages inventés par l'auteur avec un discours preliminaire*, 1767.

3 M.F. Mahony, *A Chronicle of the Fermors*, London 1873, vols I and II.

4 S. Anjou, *Marcus Gunter's Designs for Jewellery 1684-1733*, Rohsska Konstae Museum 1956, p. 43.

5 *A Book of Jeweller's Work designed by Thomas Flach*, London 1736.

6 S. Burkard, ed., *Mémoires de la Baronne d'Oberkirch*, Paris 1970, p. 169.

7 James Tassie end R.E. Raspe, *A Descriptive Catalogue of Ancient and Modern Gems taken from the most celebrated cabinets in Europe and cast in glass, enamel and sulphur etc.*, London 1791.

8 J. Grieg, ed., *Diaries of a Duchess, Extracts from the Diaries of the First Duchess of Northumberland 1716-1776*, London 1926, p. 116.

9 B. Fitzgerald, ed., *Correspondence of Emily Duchess of Leinster 1731-1814*, Dublin 1949, vol. I, p. 186.

10 W.A. Seaby, 'Objects of Vertu in the Bentinck Beresford Collection', in *The Connoisseur*, August 1955, p. 22.

11 A. Rathbone, ed., *Letters from Lady Jane Coke to her friend Mrs Eyre at Derby*, London 1899.

12 David Garrick and George Colman, *The Clandestine Marriage*, Theatre Royal, Drury Lane, 20 February 1766.

CHAPTER 3

1 Count Rudolphe Apponyi, *Vingt Cinq Ans á Paris*, Paris, 1926, vol. IV, p. 234.

2 Madame de Barrera, *Gems and Jewels*, London 1860, pp. 110-113.

3 S. Bury, 'Pugin's Marriage Jewellery', in *Victoria and Albert Museum Yearbook*, 1969, pp. 85-96.

4   D. Scarisbrick, 'The Devonshire Parure', in *Country Life*, 7 June, 1979, pp. 1796-8.

5   *Illustrated London News*, vol. 19, 1851, p. 197.

6   M. Lutyens, ed., *Effie in Venice*, London 1965, p. 138.

7   G. Munn, *Castellani and Giuliano and Revivalist Jewellers in the Nineteenth Century*, Fribourg 1983.

CHAPTER 4

1   Walburga, Lady Paget, *Embassies of Other Days*, London 1912, p. 36.

2   B. Howe, *Arbiter of Elegance*, London 1967, p. 133.

3   Lord Ronald Leveson Gower, *Old Diaries 1881-1901*, London 1902, p. 188.

4   Quoted by Yvonne Deslandres, 'Les Bijoux à la Mode au XXe Siecle', *in Métiers d'Art, September, 1983* p. 96.

5   E.G. Warwick, *Life's Ebb and Flow*, London 1929.

CHAPTER 5

1   G. Gautier, *Cartier, the Legend*, London 1983.

2   A. Selwyn, *The Retail Jeweller's Handbook*, London 1945, p. 44.

3   M. Gabardi, *Gioielli Anni '40*, Milan 1983.

4   Loelia Westminster, *Grace and Favour*, London, 1961.

5   E. Schiaparelli, *Shocking Life*, London 1954, p. 98.

6   Margaret Argyll, *Forget Not*, London, 19 _ _.

7   Earl of Carnavon, *No Regrets*, London 1976.

8   R. Gimpel, *Diary of an Art Dealer*, London, 1968, p. 122.

9   P. Hinks, *Twentieth Century British Jewellery*, London 1983, quoted p. 107.

10   C. Beaton, *The Glass of Fashion*, London 1954.

Glossary

Aiguillette a jewel terminating in a string of stones of graduated size.

A jour an open-style setting exposing all facets of a stone.

A la jeanette a peasant jewel comprising a heart with a cross attached worn from a chain or neck ribbon; traditionally a gift on the Feast of St John the Baptist.

A la porcelana an enamelled decoration on white or coloured ground, as in porcelain.

Baguette a gemstone cut so that the table or upper surface is in the form of a long narrow rectangle.

Bayardère strings of pearls twisted into a rope.

Black letter Gothic script.

Briolette a transparent elongated gemstone cut in facets with a pointed apex.

Bulla a small, hollow Roman ornament made from two concave plates.

Cabochon a gem not facetted but with the top surface rounded and polished.

Calibré cut or measured especially to fit the required shape.

Canetille filigree wire jewellery twisted into spiral patterns.

ChiRho a monogram composed of the first two letters of the name of Christ in Greek, adopted as their symbol by the early Christians.

Coulant a slide in the form of a bow, rosette, crown or heart fixed on a velvet neck ribbon with a cross in similar style attached.

Cloisonné enamel enamel divided by metal partitions fixed to a metal base.

Closed setting a gem enclosed on all sides except the top surface.

Cosses de pois a type of stylized leaf ornament based on a peapod.

Crochet a strong hook-like pin attached to brooch ornaments and chatelaines.

Email en resille sur verre a process by which a design is cut into a piece of glass or rock crystal; this is then lined with gold foil and filled with translucent enamel.

Foil a thin sheet of metal placed beneath gemstone or paste in order to enhance its brilliance or colour.

Filigree a technique of twisting and soldering thin strands of gold and silver wire into patterns.

Girandole a branch-like style of brooch or earring with three pendants hanging from a single top setting.

Guilloché enamel a transparent enamel revealing a pattern engraved on the gold surface by an engine-turning lathe.

Hung transparent hanging so that light enters the gem from all sides, unimpeded by the setting.

Lavallière a stone or pendant hanging from a fine chain.

Marcasite crystallized iron pyrites which reflects light when facetted.

Millegrain a decoration of tiny beads (grains) on the metal rim of a setting, made by a knurling tool.

Palmettes a stylized plant of classical origin with units arranged symmetrically round a central stem.

Pavé setting small stones held by claws and massed together into a mosaic pattern.

Piqué inlay of minute points or strips of gold or silver, decorating tortoiseshell or ivory.

Pinchbeck a zinc and copper alloy.

Plique à jour enamel used over an openwork design so that light strikes from front and back.

Pomander a container for scented substance carried about the person.

Reversed crystal intaglio domed crystal cut with a device, then coloured to give a three-dimensional *trompe l'oeil* effect.

Rose cut cut with 24 facets, resembling an unopened rosebud in shape.

Sautoir a long neckchain extending from the shoulders to below the waist.

Spacer a link between beads or plaques in a chain or necklace.

Sevigné a ribbon bow-knot motif.

Scots pebble quartz found in Scotland and used in jewellery.

Transparent settings a gem open at the back as well as the front.

Tremblant a jewel with motifs fitted with springs, which tremble when the wearer moves.

Torsades twisted ropes of pearls.

Select Bibliography

Becker, Vivienne, *Antique and Twentieth-century Jewellery: A Guide for Collectors*, N.A.G. Press Ltd, 1980

Bradford, Ernle, *Four Centuries of European Jewellery*, Spring Booksellers, 1953

Evans, Joan, *History of Jewellery 1100-1870*, Faber and Faber, 1970

Flower, Margaret, *Victorian Jewellery*, revised edition, Cassell, 1967

Fregnac, Claude, *Jewellery from the Renaissance to Art Nouveau*, Octopus, 1965

de Gary M.N., ed., *Les Fouquet, Bijoutiers et Joailliers à Paris 1860-1960*, Paris, 1983

Gere, Charlotte, *Victorian Jewellery Design*, Kimber, 1972

Hinks, Peter, *Nineteenth Century Jewellery*, Faber and Faber, 1975

Hinks, Peter, *Twentieth Century British Jewellery*, Faber and Faber, 1983

Lewis, M., *Antique Paste Jewellery*, Faber and Faber, 1970

Marquardt, B., *Schmuck Klaasizismus und Biedermeier 1780-1850*, Munich, 1983

Muller, P., *Jewels in Spain 1500-1800*, New York, 1972

Munn, G., *Castellani, Giuliano and Revivalist Jewellery in the Nineteenth Century*, London, 1984

Newman, Harold, *An Illustrated Dictionary of Jewellery*, Thames and Hudson, 1981

Walters Art Gallery, Baltimore, *Jewellery Ancient to Modern*, New York, 1979

Zucker, B., *Gems and Jewels, A Connoisseur's Guide*, Thames and Hudson, 1984

Index